"Becoming a church that is intentional about and effective in reaching a multicultural neighbourhood is a great but worthy challenge.

As a pastor trying to do that for my church, I found this book very helpful. It will help you discern the issues of why you should or shouldn't do it and provides you and your leaders with guidance on how to begin this journey with the church and navigate them through the challenges that come with it. I highly recommend this book to you if you are considering taking your church down this path."

Winston Mah - Minister of Merrylands Presbyterian Church, Sydney

"A great resource for both raising awareness of the need for multi-cultural ministry and for equipping workers, both professional and lay. A 'why' and 'how' manual useful for both individuals and church groups."

Trish Bell - ESL ministries co-ordinator

"I think this is the best resource out there to help pastors and churches reach this multi-ethnic city. It's based firmly in Scripture, theologically sharp. It also demonstrates not just breadth of research but depth in analysis, which serves to confront us with the challenges before us. It is clear, thorough and extremely practical. Every pastor and church would do well to work through this."

Peter Lin - Anglican Bishop of Georges River Region

"*Changing Lanes, Crossing Cultures* demystifies the cultural change taking place in our churches with guidance that is soundly biblical in its approach, helpfully practical in its structure and certainly relevant."

Steve Early - Senior Lecturer, Adelaide College of Ministries

"This book is a helpful resource and tool for churches to be challenged into effective ways of doing cross-cultural ministry. It provides a realistic insight into the many challenges faced by churches when embarking on this ministry as well as providing useful suggestions to help overcome them."

Moussa Ghazal - Minister and international student worker, Sydney

D1176294

"Three experienced practitioners have compiled an outstanding resource. This insightful book is eminently practical, empowering its readers to confidently negotiate the complex world of cross-cultural relationships. If applied carefully and prayerfully, the concepts found here will be a powerful catalyst for future change in the multi-ethnic Australian church. I recommend it wholeheartedly."

Bernie Power - Lecturer at the Melbourne School of Theology

"This is a timely and important book. Valuable because the authors are all highly experienced in the areas of cross-cultural ministry they write about.

Accessible, Biblical, and thoughtful, *Changing Lanes, Crossing Cultures* is written for churches trying to understand the culturally diverse cities and towns of Australia and looking for practical suggestions about how best to respond in ministry and mission.

I pray that its prayerful and biblical approach to cross-cultural practice and theory will generate innovative approaches to cross-cultural ministry here in Australia."

Darrell Jackson - Senior Lecturer in Missiology, Morling College, Sydney

"*Changing Lanes, Crossing Cultures* is a book for Australian churches who have a concern for their multi-cultural neighbours, but aren't sure what to do about it. The authors provide both biblical grounding and pragmatic instruction for building churches that better reflect the multi-cultural nature of our country, and the marvellous 'every tribe, language, nation and people group' nature of our heavenly home."

Simon Gillham - Head of Department of Missions, Moore Theological College

"All major Australian cities (metropolitan and regional) are now profoundly multicultural and many rural communities have their pockets of new Australians. We Christians feel that we should to reach across our local cultures but are clueless about how to start.

This book is written to help Australian churches change lanes and reach the cultures next door. The three writers bring a variety of global and local cross-cultural experiences and this enriches the book.

The book is designed to help local Australian churches understand the cultures around them and make connections for the sake of Jesus. It has a workbook format and is designed for use by groups.

The six modules cover motivations, possible barriers and methods.

A glossary and appendices including tables, diagnostic instruments and a list of resources support these modules. Individual modules typically call readers to prayer, give a Biblical reflection, provide input material for reading and end with a summary and questions to work on.

The modules are not so much a 'how-to' textbook, but rather a guide to help local churches figure out what is going on in their community and make the connections.

That's the strength of this book – it is a tool not a blueprint. Local church cultural mission is not easy and the book is frank about such challenges as motivations, practical hindrances and just getting to the first step of knowing and engaging with our neighbours. The book will push churches to look at themselves, their communities and ask the hard questions about how to connect.

This book is a timely and useful tool to help Australian churches transfer ministry wisdom from overseas mission to the local scene. It will be on my course lists."

David Burke - Lecturer in Ministry and Practice at Christ College, Sydney

Changing Lanes, Crossing Cultures

Equipping Christians and Churches for
Ministry in a Culturally Diverse Society

Andrew P. Schachtel

Choon-Hwa Lim

Michael K. Wilson

Great Western Press
Sydney - Australia

Published by Great Western Press

Copyright © 2016 Andrew P Schachtel, Choon-Hwa Lim and
Michael K Wilson
ISBN 0 86901 080 8

Apart from any fair dealing for the purposes of private study, research,
criticism or review, no part of this work may be reproduced by
electronic or other means without the permission of the authors.

Scriptures taken from Holy Bible, New International Version®, NIV®
Copyright © 1973, 1978, 1984, 2011 by Biblica, Inc® Used by
permission. All rights reserved worldwide.

Quote on page 156 is from *Cultural Intelligence: Individual Interactions
Across Cultures* by Earley, P. Christopher and Ang, Soon. Copyright
© 2003 by the Board of Trustees of the Leland Stanford Jr. University.
All rights reserved. Reprinted by permission of the publisher, Stanford
University Press, sup.org.

Illustrations by T S Lim.
Cover design and text layout by P Schachtel.

TABLE OF CONTENTS

THE WHY

THE WHAT

THE HOW

THE HOW & WHEN

LIST OF FIGURES

LIST OF TABLES

GLOSSARY

Anglo-Celtic Australian	An inhabitant of Australia who was born or whose ancestors were born in the British Isles. We use the term 'Anglo Aussie' in this book.
Cross-cultural	Comparing or dealing with two or more different cultures. Christians or churches are serving, evangelising or discipling those from differing cultural and/or ethnic backgrounds. First and second generation Christians are also often crossing cultures as they seek to minister to each other.
Cultural distance	The gap between cultures created by different ways of perceiving the world, thinking, expressing ideas, acting, interacting, communicating and making decisions.
Culture	A social phenomenon where individuals of a particular group acquire their common beliefs, values and rules of behaviour through the process of socialization at home, in the school, at work, and/or through the wider community.
Demographics	Statistical data relating to the characteristics of a population and particular groups within it.
Ethnicity	A social attribute of race that explains the diversity within and between races. People of the same ethnicity have a shared identity based on a shared history, cultural tradition, ancestry, geographic origin, language and/or other attributes that contribute to diversity.

Ethnocentrism	Evaluation of other cultures according to preconceptions originating in the standards and customs of one's own culture. Ethnocentrism is unavoidable.
First generation	We use this term to denote citizens or residents who were born overseas and have migrated to Australia.
Multi-ethnic	Consisting of, relating to, or designed for various different ethnic groups. In this book there is a particular focus on multi-ethnic churches and ministries that incorporate people from differing ethnic groups.
NESB	Non-English Speaking Background.
Organising	The structuring of people, resources, activities and workflow in the church to accomplish its goals.
Planning	The process of articulating what the church as a collective group of Bible-believers wants to do and the goals it wishes to achieve.
Racial discrimination	Behaviour and actions that treat others as inferior because of their 'race'.
Racial prejudice	The attitude or mentality that regards others as inferior because of their 'race'.
Racism	The views, practices and actions reflecting the belief that humanity is divided into distinct biological groups called 'races' and that members of a certain race share certain attributes that

| | make that group as a whole less desirable, more desirable, inferior, or superior. |

| *Second generation* | In the first instance, those in Australia who have at least one parent who migrated to Australia. However, in non-English speaking background churches even the grandchildren of such migrants may regard themselves as second generation. |

| *Strategic plan* | Strategic planning involves articulating a vision and mission, a plan to realise this vision and the resources to action the plan. |

| *SWOT* | In this book, SWOT is a structured planning method used to evaluate the Strengths, Weaknesses, Opportunities, and Threats of a project or venture involving ministry across cultures. |

| *TESL* | Teaching of English as a Second Language. |

| *Worldview* | A collection of beliefs about life, the universe and the nature of reality held by an individual or a group. |

FOREWORD

Around six million Australians were born overseas, and approximately five million speak a language other than English at home. While some people who have come from overseas have a vibrant Christian faith, many do not know Christ. Among them are more than a million Buddhists, Hindus, and Muslims. How can Australian Christians and churches help these people hear and experience the good news that God loves them and is inviting them into his kingdom? This book addresses this question in particularly practical way. If your church needs help in reaching out to people from ethnic minorities in your neighbourhood, this book is for you!

The authors are not just theoreticians. They write out of decades of personal experience in reaching out to people from cultures other than their own, both overseas and in Australia. This means that what you have in your hands is an intensely practical handbook. It clearly explains the why, what, how, and when of reaching people from other cultures with the gospel and helping them become part of your church. But this is not only a practical book; it is also thoroughly biblical. Every chapter begins by leading readers through the biblical foundations that undergird each aspect of cross-cultural ministry.

Cross-cultural ministry is challenging. Many of us are afraid of what we do not understand. We are reticent to tread on other people's "cultural toes." The authors understand this, and lead us on a journey of discovery. They help us to first to discover what might be hindering us or our church from reaching people from other cultures. They then address some of these hindrances by enabling readers to see how cultural differences affect relationships. Building on this, they lead us along a pathway of practical steps that we can take to launch into this work.

Thousands of people from ethnic minorities in Australia remain outside the reach of the gospel. They have never had the chance to hear the good news in a way they understand. As followers of Jesus we have the great privilege of befriending them, introducing them to the King of Kings, and welcoming them into the church. This book is a particularly helpful guide to engaging in this vital task.

DR RICHARD HIBBERT

DIRECTOR OF THE SCHOOL OF CROSS-CULTURAL MISSION,
SYDNEY MISSIONARY & BIBLE COLLEGE

PREFACE

We have written this book to help Australian Christians and churches, regardless of their ethnic backgrounds, to see the urgent need to reach out fruitfully across cultures. We prefer to speak of 'fruitful' rather than 'successful', bearing in mind that we glorify God as, abiding in Christ, we bear much fruit (John 15:8). We see churches as being fruitful when, regardless of size, they are truly loving, Christlike communities and when they are profoundly committed to communicating the Gospel within and across cultures.

 **ANDREW SCHACHTEL** was the Director of CultureConnect, Interserve's ministry among people of other faiths and ethnic backgrounds living in Australia. He continues to minister amongst migrants, refugees and international students. Andrew worked overseas with Interserve for more than 20 years, mostly in countries where Buddhism is the major religion. Through CultureConnect, he enjoys helping Australian Christians see the many opportunities to reach out cross-culturally in their own 'backyard' and train them in general cross-cultural skills and understanding minority faiths, with a particular interest in Buddhism. Andrew set up a website that supports, links and resources Christians working cross-culturally around Australia (*www.cultureconnect.net.au*).

Andrew is married to Muriel. They live in Wollongong and are active members of the multi-ethnic local Baptist Church, where Andrew is the ministry co-ordinator for re-settler support.

CHOON-HWA LIM is Malaysian-born Chinese, educated in New Zealand and Australia, and now lives in Sydney with her family.

After two decades of working in industry locally and overseas, she earned a PhD from Macquarie University where she was adjunct lecturer in Cross Cultural Management. Choon-Hwa is now a practising psychologist in mental health, and teaches Intercultural Communication for CAPA The Global Education Network. Her website is *www.psychology.org.au/Lim*

Passionate about helping Christians and churches engage across cultures, Choon-Hwa developed the International Ministry at Christ Church Anglican Church, St Ives, served on the Sydney Anglican Northern Region Multicultural Ministry Committee, and is currently supporting a Presbyterian multicultural church plant in Sydney's West. Over the last eight years she has been consulting with churches, working across the denominations.

MIKE WILSON is married to Barbara. They have three daughters and a son, all now married and growing Christian families of their own.

Following seven years of missionary service in Pakistan, Mike has been helping churches to reach out to people across cultures in Australia and abroad. Mike is an ordained Presbyterian minister and served as the Cross Cultural Ministry Coordinator for the Presbyterian Church of NSW. He is now a Regional Ministry Director for SIM Australia.

Mike has lectured at Christ College, Sydney Missionary and Bible College, Wesley Institute, Moore Theological College and the Brisbane School of Theology. Subject areas include Old Testament, Multicultural Ministry and a Christian Understanding of Buddhism. Mike's resources can be found on his website at *www.facetofaceintercultural.com.au*.

The authors have enjoyed working together in the writing of this book, at times working through and benefiting from our differences. We are from different denominations. We were all born in different countries with different ethnic roots and very different prior cross-cultural experience. We have all wrestled with cultural issues and share a vision and passion to motivate Australian Christians and churches to do what they can to ensure all people are given the opportunity to know the love of Christ, regardless of their ethnic or cultural background.

Perhaps you and your church have not seriously considered reaching out across cultures. Or perhaps you are initiating such a ministry or even seeking to improve it. This book is written for such Christians and churches in Australia, whatever their ethnic or cultural background. We realise that alternative approaches are often needed for non-Anglo Aussie churches, though we believe that the book will still be relevant for them. Most of the contents of this book are relevant for any Christian with a heart and vision for such ministry. We would love everyone, regardless of their roles, but including those in a variety of formal leadership positions, to consider how to use this material to promote such a heart and vision.

This book is designed so that any person can pick it up and read it. However, we have particularly sought to produce a book that many will want to study in groups. If you are studying it in a group, we recommend that you do so over six sessions, as follows:

Session 1   Introduction & Module 1 (The Unchanging Fuel)

Session 2   Module 2 (Changing Road Conditions)

Session 3   Module 3 (Changing Road Responses)

Session 4   Module 4 (Changing Driver Skills)

Session 5   Module 5 (Changing Road Management)

Session 6   Module 6 & Conclusion (Changing the GPS)

Modules 2, 3, 4, 5 and 6 begin with a biblical reflection which readers may want to work through prior to reading the module. Appendix A contains further notes on these reflections.

We recommend that you read the relevant section/s before each session, then come prepared to discuss the section/s and the questions that follow them. And, we encourage you to include eating together as part of your discussion group meetings! We are willing to assist in facilitating these sessions, consulting and running workshops and seminars.

From time to time we make reference to what is happening in particular churches, though without naming them. We want to avoid criticising any particular church or making any suggestion that a particular church provides a perfect or ideal model — instead we seek to learn from the experience of such churches. Any examples we provide are from actual churches and merely illustrate particular points.

We also include a number of case studies. These are included to illustrate points being made in the text, or to stimulate your thinking about possible courses of action. Names used in the case studies and stories are fictitious, but are based on real people and situations.

ACKNOWLEDGEMENTS

In writing this book, we would like to acknowledge the contributions of many people, including:

The 19 cross-cultural practitioners who gave us valuable feedback on the draft text.

Nita Kambouris for her helpful advice on the demographic data in Appendix B.

T. S. Lim for his line drawings.

Peter Schachtel for preparing the layout and design.

Our spouses, for their inputs and patience as we worked on the book.

The authors would especially like to thank Interserve Australia for sponsoring this book.

 **Interserve**

INTRODUCTION - WHOM & WHAT THIS BOOK IS FOR

The authors of this book are seeking to encourage and help Christians and churches to reach ethnic minorities in Australia. This book is about the WHY, WHAT, HOW and WHEN of vibrant cross-cultural ministries.

We are not thinking merely of first generation migrants when we speak of ethnic minorities — those who were born in another land but have now settled in Australia, many of whom are fluent English-speakers but some with little or no English. We are also thinking of many second generation migrants, those with first generation parentage but who themselves were born in Australia, though here we include the '1.5ers', those born overseas but raised in Australia from a very early age.

When we speak of churches reaching ethnic minorities, we are not thinking merely of churches that have traditionally been Anglo Aussie and may still be dominantly Anglo Aussie in composition or in leadership. We are calling all churches, irrespective of their ethnic or cultural background, to take seriously this matter of reaching out to ethnic minorities.

There are many fascinating and challenging considerations to address in seeking to develop ministry across cultural and ethnic boundaries. Here is a sample of questions a church may well have to address (see Appendix C for a fuller listing):

1. In churches where leaders are in earnest about developing ministry across cultures, how can church members who are used to a long-established model of church based on the dominant culture be helped to see the need for the church to reach out to people cross-culturally?

2. How can church members be helped to understand people of other cultures so as to avoid hurtful misunderstandings and to value people on their own terms?

3. How can supportive structures for ministry across cultures be developed both within the church community and the denomination of which the church may be a part?

4. In a church where the composition of the membership is becoming more ethnically diverse, how should leadership structures be developed that are not dominated by the majority culture of church members?

5. How can we go about understanding the specific needs of ethnic minorities in our particular community, and how do we assess the effectiveness of our outreach efforts?

By now, you'll have some idea of the complexities of developing an effective cross-cultural ministry that honours God. However, the challenges are not insurmountable. In a sense, this is not unlike drivers trying to navigate through heavy traffic to safely change lanes!

Who is this book for?

This book is designed to help you and your church recognise some of these challenges, begin training in the appropriate skills, and launch into appropriate engagement and ministry among people from a wide range of ethnic backgrounds.

CHANGING LANES - STEERING CHURCHES INTO MINISTRY ACROSS CULTURES

Good drivers don't stay in the right-hand lane when you are trying to overtake them. Good drivers use their rear-vision mirrors. Some churches are good at spotting the demographic changes that are looming up behind them and they adjust well. They are not pigheadedly refusing to budge. Ethnocentrism and racism do not cause them to close their ears to the blaring horns of biblical truth and social reality that are pressing them to move. No! They are willing to change, to reach out to the ethnic minorities that are increasingly becoming part of the communities in which they are located.

Good drivers will check their rear-vision mirrors and flash their indicators before changing lanes. They don't drive recklessly or as though they own the road. They remain alert to what other cars around them are doing. Good drivers are conscious of 'the blind spot'. So when they are about to change lanes they not only check side mirrors and the rear-vision mirrors, they also turn their heads. It is always heartening to see churches prepare themselves properly before they launch into ministry across cultures. Instead of acting autonomously such churches tap valuable external expertise. They learn from experienced churches, and they seek to coordinate their ministry initiatives with what others are already doing.

Drivers find themselves sharing the road with such vehicles as cars, trucks, buses, bicycles, motorcycles and caravans. Good drivers adjust their driving practices accordingly, even if this means drivers are not free to drive as they might otherwise do. Similarly, churches ministering across cultures make necessary adjustments to cater for the different ethnicities and cultures of people. They avoid the assimilationist mindset ('cultural imperialism') that assumes that all people will simply adapt to the culture of their church.

Good drivers don't drink before they drive. It is crucial to be aware of what other drivers are doing on the road and be able to properly judge distances between vehicles. Intoxication deadens such senses. Churches act soberly when they are able to properly assess the significance of cultural distance. They don't become intoxicated with the wrong-headed notion that there is a standard gospel 'size', and accepted communication methods, that will fit all.

Coming together

Good drivers avoid excess speed, mindful of how often this contributes to serious accidents. When churches are ministering across cultures they are well advised to avoid implementing major new ventures too rapidly. Some minor bumps and scrapes may occur. But serious 'crashes' can cause a lot of hurt and pain and lead churches to react negatively to ministry across cultures. So, from time to time, one comes across some who say, "We tried that and it didn't work," as though that justified discarding any prospect of engaging in ministry across cultures in the future.

In different cultures drivers may use the same signals to mean different things. In some cultures the use of a car's indicator does not mean, "I am about to change lanes," but "You can now overtake me." When churches are 'changing lanes' cross-culturally they need to make sure that communication of what they are doing makes sense to those involved — not merely to majority culture church members, but also to minority culture Christians.

Good drivers adapt their driving to different driving conditions and road surfaces. They slow down on wet surfaces and in heavy fog. They take extra precautions when driving on gravel or ice or roads dotted with potholes. Churches that are competent in ministering across cultures are similarly sensitive to the sometimes very different cultural contexts they encounter.

We hope that this book will help you and your church to become good drivers in our increasingly multi-ethnic country.

THE WHY

Module 1

THE UNCHANGING FUEL: BIBLICAL MOTIVATION FOR MINISTRY ACROSS CULTURES

1.1 Prayer | 1.2 Introduction | 1.3 Biblical motivation
1.4 Christlike motivation | 1.5 Demographic motivation
1.6 Motivation to combat ungodly obstacles
1.7 Motivation from considering the benefits
1.8 Summary | 1.9 Questions

1.1 Prayer

1.2 Introduction

Good drivers get to their destinations safely and on time. To do so, good drivers ensure that their vehicles are powered by the right type and amount of fuel. Christians and churches can be topped up with the right fuel by looking to the One who calls us to treat foreigners as native-born and not to mistreat them (Leviticus 19:33-34).

1.3 Biblical motivation

William Carey (1761–1834), so called 'father of modern mission', had much to do with making Matthew's Great Commission a primary source of motivation for ministry across cultures. Here we read:

> Then Jesus came to them and said, "All authority in heaven and on earth has been given to me. Therefore go and make disciples of all nations, baptizing them in the name of the Father and of the Son and of the Holy Spirit, and teaching them to obey everything I have commanded you. And surely I am with you always, to the very end of the age."
>
> MATTHEW 28:18-20

There are many other biblical perspectives we can draw on in urging churches to reach out across cultures. Indeed, central to the entire sweep of biblical thought is a progressive movement, climaxing in the work of Christ, which involves the creation of a new multi-ethnic humanity in God's image and likeness in a new heaven and a new earth. It would take a book to do justice to this! Here are some biblical anchors for such a ministry:

A. Human dignity

> Then God said, 'Let us make mankind in our image, in our likeness, so that they may rule over the fish in the sea and the birds in the sky, over the livestock and all the wild animals, and over all the creatures that move along the ground.' So God created mankind in his own image, in the image of God he created them; male and female he created them.
>
> GENESIS 1:26-27

> When I consider your heavens, the work of your fingers, the moon and the stars, which you have set in place, what is mankind that you are mindful of them, human beings that you care for them? You have made them a little lower than the angels and crowned them

with glory and honour. You made them rulers over the works of your hands; you put everything under their feet: all flocks and herds, and the animals of the wild, the birds in the sky, and the fish in the sea, all that swim the paths of the seas.

PSALM 8:3-8

From one man he made all the nations, that they should inhabit the whole earth…

ACTS 17:26

With the tongue we praise our Lord and Father, and with it we curse human beings, who have been made in God's likeness.

JAMES 3:9

QUESTIONS

1. What biblical and other considerations motivate you to respect all people?

2. Does our knowledge of people's essential dignity move us to reach out across cultures? Why or why not?

Truth: All people share the same glorious origin. All are created in the image of God. This motivates us to treat people from all cultures and ethnic backgrounds with profound respect and try to reach out to them.

B. Human perversity

We all, like sheep, have gone astray, each of us has turned to our own way; and the LORD has laid on him the iniquity of us all.

ISAIAH 53:6

… for all have sinned and fall short of the glory of God…

ROMANS 3:23

The heart is deceitful above all things and beyond cure. Who can understand it?

JEREMIAH 17:9

For the wages of sin is death, but the gift of God is eternal life in Christ Jesus our Lord.

ROMANS 6:23

QUESTIONS

1. What biblical and other considerations indicate that all people are indeed radically sinful and doomed?

2. Does our knowledge of people's desperate situation move us to reach out across cultures? Why or why not?

Truth: As James 3:9 indicates (see above), the Fall has not resulted in the image of God being obliterated, but sin is dehumanising. All people, regardless of their ethnic or cultural background, being inescapably sinful, are biased against God. Death, the wages of sin, does not discriminate between people. Apart from divine intervention, all people regardless of their ethnic or cultural background face the prospect of eternal separation from God. God does not want anyone to perish ("The Lord is not slow in keeping his promise, as some understand slowness. Instead he is patient with you, not wanting anyone to perish, but everyone to come to repentance." 2 Peter 3:9) and nor should we. This motivates us to have compassion on all lost people, whatever their cultural or ethnic background.

C. Collective evil

Now the whole world had one language and a common speech. As people moved eastward, they found a plain in Shinar and settled there. They said to each other, 'Come, let's make bricks and bake them thoroughly.' They used brick instead of stone, and tar for mortar. Then they said, 'Come, let us build ourselves a city, with a tower that reaches to the heavens, so that we may make a name for ourselves; otherwise we will be scattered over the face of the whole earth.' But the Lord came down to see the city and the tower the people were building. The Lord said, 'If as one people speaking the same language they have begun to do this, then nothing they plan to do will be impossible for them. Come, let us go down and confuse their language so they will not understand each other.' So the Lord scattered them from there over all the earth, and they stopped building the city. That is why it was called Babel—because there the Lord confused the language of the whole world. From there the Lord scattered them over the face of the whole earth.

GENESIS 11:1-9

Why do the nations conspire and the peoples plot in vain? The kings of the earth rise up and the rulers band together against the Lord and against his anointed, saying, 'Let us break their chains and throw off their shackles.'

PSALM 2:1-3

But when the apostles Barnabas and Paul heard of this, they tore their clothes and rushed out into the crowd, shouting: 'Friends, why are you doing this? We too are only human, like you. We are bringing you good news, telling you to turn from these worthless things to the living God, who made the heavens and the earth and the sea and everything in them. In the past, he let all nations go their own way.'

ACTS 14:14-16

QUESTIONS

1. What do you admire in your own and other cultures?

2. What biblical and other considerations convince you that, in and of themselves, people are incapable of acting collectively to produce societies and cultures that honour the Lord?

3. In what ways does the gospel call into question your own culture?

Truth: Given their sinful bias, people, in and of themselves, are incapable of behaving collectively to develop societies and cultures that honour God — as the Tower of Babel episode illustrates. Just as nobility and goodness are still to be found in the lives of sinful people, so culture too contains much that is laudable. Nevertheless, in their sinfulness people not only individually but also collectively reject God's will for their lives and go their own way. So the way of life people construct for their societies inevitably involves replacing God with other things. Consequently, culture, like people, is also biased against God. We must expect that the gospel will call upon us, and the people we are seeking to win for Christ, to change our way of life in key respects.

D. The new humanity

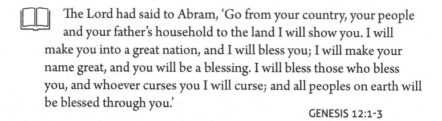

The Lord had said to Abram, 'Go from your country, your people and your father's household to the land I will show you. I will make you into a great nation, and I will bless you; I will make your name great, and you will be a blessing. I will bless those who bless you, and whoever curses you I will curse; and all peoples on earth will be blessed through you.'

GENESIS 12:1-3

Is this blessedness (of justification and forgiveness) only for the circumcised, or also for the uncircumcised? We have been saying that Abraham's faith was credited to him as righteousness. Under what circumstances was it credited? Was it after he was circumcised, or before? It was not after, but before! And he received circumcision as a sign, a seal of the righteousness that he had by faith while he was still uncircumcised. So then, he is the father of all who believe but have not been circumcised, in order that righteousness might be credited to them. And he is then also the father of the circumcised who not only are circumcised but who also follow in the footsteps of the faith that our father Abraham had before he was circumcised.

ROMANS 4:9-12

But now in Christ Jesus you who once were far away have been brought near by the blood of Christ. For he himself is our peace, who has made the two groups (Jews and Gentiles) one and has destroyed the barrier, the dividing wall of hostility, by setting aside in his flesh the law with its commands and regulations. His purpose was to create in himself one new humanity out of the two, thus making peace, and in one body to reconcile both of them to God through the cross, by which he put to death their hostility. He came and preached peace to you who were far away and peace to those who were near. For through him we both have access to the Father by one Spirit.

EPHESIANS 2:13-18

After this I looked, and there before me was a great multitude that no one could count, from every nation, tribe, people and language, standing before the throne and before the Lamb. They were wearing white robes and were holding palm branches in their hands. And they cried out in a loud voice: 'Salvation belongs to our God, who sits on the throne, and to the Lamb.'

REVELATION 7:9-10

QUESTIONS

1. How does knowledge of God's fundamental commitment to forming a new humanity help you to understand human history?

2. What biblical and other perspectives help you to understand how God might want us to contribute to the development of this new humanity?

3. In what ways can and does your church reflect God's heart to bring people from all cultural, ethnic and linguistic backgrounds into his eternal kingdom?

Truth: Given the universal corruption of humanity, God called Abraham to be the head of a new humanity. God alone creates a true humanity that relates to him rightly. God began to work out this purpose through the Jewish people. But the Abrahamic promises are aimed at developing a new humanity that is composed of all who relate to God with Abraham-like faith, whether Jews or non-Jews (Gentiles). Through Christ's sacrificial death God has reconciled Jew and Gentile in the sphere of the new humanity, the church. Indeed, ultimately this new humanity will be a vast united body of people "from every nation, tribe, people and language." This international community will forever be in awe of the way God has brought about their salvation through the sacrifice of the Lamb of God. We are motivated by this to share the Lord's commitment to uniting people from all ethnic, cultural and linguistic backgrounds.

E. The work of Christ

Jews demand signs and Greeks look for wisdom, but we preach Christ crucified: a stumbling block to Jews and foolishness to Gentiles, but to those whom God has called, both Jews and Greeks, Christ the power of God and the wisdom of God.

1 CORINTHIANS 1:22-24

There is no difference between Jew and Gentile, for all have sinned and fall short of the glory of God, and all are justified freely by his grace through the redemption that came by Christ Jesus.

ROMANS 3:22B-24

If you declare with your mouth, 'Jesus is Lord', and believe in your heart that God raised him from the dead, you will be saved. For it is with your heart that you believe and are justified, and it is with your mouth that you profess your faith and are saved. As Scripture says, 'Anyone who believes in him will never be put to shame.' For there is no difference between Jew and Gentile—the same Lord is Lord of all and richly blesses all who call on him, for, 'Everyone who calls on the name of the Lord will be saved.'

ROMANS 10:9-13

For God so loved the world that he gave his one and only Son, that whoever believes in him shall not perish but have eternal life.

JOHN 3:16

He (Jesus) is the atoning sacrifice for our sins, and not only for ours but also for the sins of the whole world.

1 JOHN 2:2

And they sang a new song, saying: 'You are worthy to take the scroll and to open its seals, because you were slain, and with your blood you purchased for God persons from every tribe and language and people and nation.'

REVELATION 5:9

Truth: Jesus did not die on the cross merely to bring about the salvation of his Jewish compatriots but so that people from every conceivable ethnic, cultural and linguistic background might be called into his kingdom. We desire that all should share our own sense of wonderment at the enormity of what Christ has suffered for us and achieved for us.

QUESTIONS

1. What does the death and resurrection of Jesus achieve for all whom God calls?

2. Can you give some examples of cultural ways of thinking and behaving that hamper people's ability to grasp the significance of what happened on the cross?

There are many other biblical perspectives that might move us and our churches to reach out across ethnic, cultural and linguistic divides.

1.4 Christlike motivation

But motivation involves more than an intellectual understanding of the biblical reasons for engaging in such ministry, as important as this undoubtedly is. While obedience is certainly a valid motive, we do not major on motivating churches to do this ministry out of a sense of guilt. In *Let The Nations Be Glad*, John Piper (2010, pp. 36, 255) stresses the foundational importance of worship to taking the gospel across cultures. He reminds us that worship "is the fuel and goal of missions"; that "Missions begins and ends in worship"; and that "Where passion for God is weak, zeal for missions will be weak".

" If the halter is on the horse and one can get hold of it and turn
the horse's head, the rest of the horse will follow. So too with
human beings. Once God gets hold of a person's heart, the renovation
of the whole person has been set in motion. When the heart is led in a
particular direction, the rest will follow." (Witherington III 2009, p. 32).

BEN WITHERINGTON III B. 1951
AMERICAN NEW TESTAMENT SCHOLAR

It is in worship, the contemplation of the glory of God in the face of Christ,
that we are transformed into the likeness of Christ by the Spirit (2 Corinthians 3:18; cf. 4:6). It is Christlike to look with compassion on the mul-
titudes of those who are "like sheep without a shepherd" (Matthew 9:36).
It is Christlike to be moved when realising that the harvest is great but the
labourers few (v37). It is Christlike to pray to the Lord of the harvest to
send out labourers into the harvest field (v38). Don't be surprised if, as
Jesus' own disciples soon discovered (Matthew 10:1ff), the Lord sends us
out in answer to such prayer.

QUESTIONS

1. What might you do
to strengthen your
own commitment to
developing a Christlike
heart for the lost people
of all cultures?

2. How can you help
fellow Christians and
your church to develop
mission-engendering
worship and prayer?

In short, motivation for ministry
across cultures involves more than
mere intellectual understanding of
biblical teaching. It also presupposes
that we are developing loving Christlike hearts for the nations as we engage
in worship and prayer.

1.5 Demographic Motivation

Given our conviction as to the sover-
eignty of our Lord, we do not regard it as a mere accident of history that
the nations are coming to Australia. Coming to terms with statistical facts
played a key role in two major turning points in the history of missions:
the commencement of the modern missionary movement and the begin-
ning of inland missions. William Carey was not merely moved by the Great

Commission but also by his thorough study of Captain Cook's journals and his attempt to calculate how many people in each part of the world were without Christ. Hudson Taylor, the founder of the China Inland Mission (now OMF), which led to the formation of other inland missions, refused to stay on the coast where other missionaries were serving because he was so profoundly moved by his understanding that the masses of China lived in the interior. It is now time for us to allow demographic realities to impress upon us the urgency of the need for ministry across cultures and to alert us to the golden opportunities sitting on our doorsteps. The extent of Australia's ethnic diversity is the subject of Appendix B.

Consider the vast numbers of international students who are studying in Australia at any one point of time. Indeed, in its 2014 message to international students, the Council of International Students Australia (CISA, http://cisa.edu.au) claimed to be speaking for about 450,000 students in Australia. It is a sad fact that the vast majority of all such students, who sometimes spend years in Australia, never enter the home of an Australian citizen and never have any significant Christian contact. Yet many of these students on returning to their home countries will take up a wide range of strategic leadership positions. What a tragedy it will be if Christians in Australia miss this golden opportunity to show warm Christian hospitality and to impact other nations!

1.6 Motivation to Combat Ungodly Obstacles

Because ungodly or unbiblical reasons often stand in the way of developing appropriate ministries to reach ethnic minorities, it is helpful to bear in mind some additional biblical and theological considerations:

Before Jesus presented the Parable of the Good Samaritan he had told an expert in the law what he must do in order to inherit eternal life, namely to love God with every fibre of his being and love his neighbour as himself (Luke 10:25-28). In response, the expert in the law hoped to justify himself, to reassure himself that he had sufficiently complied with this demand, by taking the command to love one's neighbour and cutting it down to a size he could manage. Hence the question, "Who is my neighbour?" In other words, if he can limit the definition of 'neighbour' in a manner acceptable to himself, then he can rest easier. Jesus' parable teaches that there is no limit to the understanding of who might be one's 'neighbour'. Why, it even includes those upon whom we tend to look down, or one's dire enemy! It follows from this that Christians and churches are acting like the expert in the law if they justify their failure to reach out to ethnic minorities (and others) in need by effectively limiting their definition of those they will consider as their neighbour.

The good samaritan

Jesus portrays the community of his disciples as the salt of the earth and the light of the world. At the very least this implies that the church must be an attractive community. In suburbs where there are high percentages of people from ethnic minorities it is to be expected that some will simply walk into church services or come to the church playgroup. If such visitors are genuinely viewed as neighbours, then members of the church will do all they can to welcome them and help meet their needs, or to provide them with meaningful engagement with the church as co-labourers for the same cause.

The person who loves their dream of community will destroy community, but the person who loves those around them will create community." (Bonhoeffer 1965, pp. 15-16).

DIETRICH BONHOEFFER (1906-1945)
GERMAN THEOLOGIAN

A. Christians are exhorted to do good to everyone (Galatians 6:10a), so church members will seek to welcome, understand and meet the needs of all such people who come to the church, whether from the same or different cultures.

> Miriam was a recent migrant from mainland China. She started coming regularly to the ESL class run by a local church. After class Miriam approached the teacher in a distressed state. Given her limited English she needed help from other group members to get across the gist of her situation. She explained that her husband was threatening to leave her and take their child with him. The teacher was able to consult with another member of her church who found a Mandarin speaker to communicate more fully with Miriam. In this way the church was able to put her in touch with authorities able to advise her as to her options and legal rights. The Mandarin-speaking church member and his wife were able to meet with the husband and wife together and effect some measure of reconciliation. Miriam has since become a believer.

B. Christians are urged to do good, especially "to those who belong to the family of believers." (Galatians 6:10b). So even greater efforts must be expended to understand and meet the needs of Christians from ethnic minorities who come to the church. "This is how we know what love is: Jesus Christ laid down his life for us. And we ought to lay down our lives for our brothers and sisters. If anyone has material possessions and sees a brother or sister in need but has no pity on them, how can the love of God be that person? Dear children, let us not love with words or tongue but with actions and in truth." 1 John 3:16-18

C. Christians must not show partiality with respect to those who come into the church assembly (James 2:1-13): "My brothers, as believers in our glorious Lord Jesus Christ, don't show favouritism... If you really keep the royal law found in Scripture, 'Love your neighbour as your-self,' you are doing right. But if you show favouritism, you sin and are convicted by the law as lawbreakers... Speak and act as those who are going to be judged by the law that gives freedom, because judgment without mercy will be shown to anyone who has not been merciful. Mercy triumphs over judgment!" James 2:1, 8-9, 12-13

Sadly, professing Christians don't always demonstrate sensitivity to the needs of Christians from ethnic minorities. A certain suburban church permitted a South American congregation to share its facilities. There were some initial efforts on the part of the pastor of this church to seek to incorporate the South American pastor and his congregation into the church community. The South American congregation was youthful, had good musicians and expensive musical equipment. The host church required them to pack up most of their equipment after each service. But the pastor did give permission for some things to be left ready for use. However, despite this, time and again members of the host congregation complained and packed up these items. The South American congregation eventually decided that using the church building for its services was too much hassle, and opted to use the hall instead. Their sense of being unwelcome and at best second-class members of the church was heightened when, on a number of occasions, members of the host congregation openly voiced their dissatisfaction to members of the South American congregation. The members of the South American congregation could not enjoy their association with this church and felt they were always walking on eggshells. Eventually, they decided to relocate.

1.7 Motivation from Considering the Benefits

Megan Presbury said in *ESL Classes Reveal Buried Treasure*, "I've heard from a lot of churches that the mission focus of our ESL programs has often reinvigorated the church community in their attitude towards mission. Many who served in ESL ministry have also told me that actively putting their faith into action in this way strengthens their own walk and crystallises their faith." (Wilson 2008).

A number of positive benefits result from engaging in ministry to people from other ethnic and cultural backgrounds:

A. For some church members who become involved in such a ministry this is their first significant ministry commitment and the first major use of their spiritual gifts. Church members who were previously little more than pew-sitters are suddenly revitalised and their enthusiasm is infectious.

> Leng is a shy Chinese Singaporean Christian who attended a largely Anglo church. Her husband will not come to church. She didn't know anyone in the church and would just come to the church service and then leave. Leng, who speaks English well was invited to help with the church's English conversation classes with migrant peoples. Life took on new meaning for Leng who, despite her busy life, is fully involved in this ministry. She has become a vitally plugged-in member of the church who is diligent in following-up those who come to the classes. From time to time she speaks to the congregation about the importance of this ministry.

B. Especially with wise and careful training, church members develop a clearer grasp of the gospel and basic Christian theology as they find themselves having to articulate fundamental concepts in simple terms to those who have had limited or no exposure to Christianity in the countries from which they came and/or for whom English may be a second or third language.

> Fran is an Anglo Aussie who has been part of a denominational church for most of her life. She was a long-standing member of the church's women's group, but she was a 'milk Christian' who did not feed on the meat of God's work. When she decided to help with the church's outreach program to migrant peoples she came to all the training sessions. She has grown 'leaps and bounds' in her spiritual life. Previously, she would never have been prepared to teach the Bible to others. Now she is committed to the power of the gospel and does teach the Bible to migrant people who come to the church, despite being 'just an ordinary member' of her church.

C. This ministry provides the opportunity to serve others (Galatians 6:9-10), both spiritually and physically. Many migrants who become part of Australia's ethnic minorities have great unmet needs, e.g. traumatic past experiences, the experience of culture shock/stress, acute loneliness, dislocation from loved ones, inability to communicate, loss of identity, difficulties in finding employment, and fears that their children will be seriously damaged by certain aspects of Australian culture, etc.

> Sylvia remembers how wrenching an experience it was when, as a young married Anglo Aussie woman, she moved from Melbourne to Brisbane. Her church in Brisbane talked about starting a ministry to migrants. She became involved in this when she realized the even greater experiences of dislocation many of them had experienced.

D. This ministry facilitates the development of loving relationships. Many church members who become involved in such ministries testify to the deep love the Lord instils in their hearts for the people to whom they minister.

> Jim met Bosnian refugee Dragan at a soccer game. Jim discovered that Dragan's son and his son both played for the same team. In conversation he learned that Dragan and his wife Dina wanted to improve their English and find their place in Australian society. Jim offered to help them with their English and most weeks met with them for this purpose. Dragan had been a successful dentist in Bosnia but was unable to meet the conditions for becoming a dentist in Australia. Through his friendship with Dragan and Dina, Jim gained insight into the plight faced by many refugees and developed a heart for ministering to them.

E. The church community grows in its authenticity and credibility before a sceptical and critical world as it demonstrates in highly practical and tangible ways that the gospel indeed is for all peoples regardless of ethnic, cultural and linguistic differences, and that the church can truly be a healthy and vibrant multi-ethnic community.

> Julian the Apostate was the Roman emperor from AD 361-363. He was opposed to Christians, whom he referred to as 'Galileans'. It is ironic to read one of his complaints against Christians: "These impious Galileans not only feed their own poor, but ours also; welcoming them into their *agape*, they attract them, as children are attracted, with cakes ... Whilst the pagan priests neglect the poor, the hated Galileans devote themselves to works of charity and by a display of false compassion have established and given effect to their pernicious errors ..."
>
> *(Source: Letter to Arsacius, high priest of Galatia, AD 362)*

F.   Endeavouring to enfold people from ethnic minorities into the life of the church causes church members to come to grips with what is really fundamental with respect to developing God-honouring unity.

...for all of you who were baptized into Christ have clothed yourselves with Christ. There is neither Jew nor Gentile, neither slave nor free, nor is there male and female, for you are all one in Christ Jesus. If you belong to Christ, then you are Abraham's seed, and heirs according to the promise.

GALATIANS 3: 27-29

G.   This ministry helps church members to learn that their primary quest is that of "seeking first the kingdom of God and his righteousness" (Matthew 6:33), since many of those won for Christ or ministered to in such contexts may eventually find their way into other churches (e.g. own-language churches). This results in kingdom growth rather than the numerical growth of the ministering church's community.

H.   God's people are called upon to seek the welfare of the society in which they live (e.g. Jeremiah 29:7; Romans 13:1-7; 1 Timothy 2:1-4). By bringing culturally diverse people together in a caring context, church-based ministries to ethnic minorities are making a significant contribution towards social cohesion, and helping to address racist attitudes.

In his book *People of the Dream*, Christian sociologist Michael Emerson (2006, pp. 160-164) observes that multi-ethnic churches are typically more diverse than their neighbourhoods. They are also typically more economically mixed than homogenous churches. Emerson's research into American churches revealed that in homogeneous churches 86% of members say most of their friends share the same ethnic background, whereas in multi-ethnic churches only 25% say this.

1.8 Summary

A vision and passion for ministry across cultures will grow as we develop biblical convictions and become more like Jesus in the way we look at others. We need God's word to motivate us to combat and overcome obstacles in godly ways, so that we can respond effectively to the demographic realities around us, and reflect God's design for humanity.

Module 2 explores aspects of Australia's ethnic diversity, and the implications for ministry.

1.9 Questions

1. Which passages from the Bible have served to move you to minister across cultures?

2. What are some other biblical truths or considerations that God has used in your life or in that of others to motivate ministry across cultures?

3. Reflect on Piper's (2010, p. 255) contention that "Mission begins and ends in worship." What implications does this have for your personal commitment and your church's commitment to mission or ministry across cultures?

4. Which of the motivating factors outlined in this module particularly resonate with you?

5. Not only in churches but also in the secular world various efforts are made to serve people from other cultures. What motivations, apart from those considered in this module, might explain such endeavours?

6. Following on from the previous question, what are healthy reasons for engaging in ministry across cultures and what are unhealthy reasons?

7. What can and should be done to address any levels of complacency, apathy and inertia among the members of your church towards ministry across cultures?

8. Apart from structured church services, what opportunities are there in your church for members to worship the Lord together and in that context to develop a Christlike heart for people from other cultures?

(?)

Notes

_____

_____

_____

_____

_____

_____

_____

_____

_____

_____

_____

_____

_____

_____

_____

_____

_____

_____

_____

Module 2

CHANGING ROAD CONDITIONS: MINISTRY IN AN ETHNICALLY DIVERSE SOCIETY

2.1 Prayer

2.2 Introduction

 ... our culture may tell us where we've come from, our identity in the family of God tells us where we are going." (Rhodes 1998, p. 45).

STEPHEN RHODES (B.1960)
AMERICAN CHRISTIAN AUTHOR

From your own observations and from reading Appendix B, you'll be in no doubt that Australia is a very multi-ethnic country. A large proportion of our population was born overseas, millions routinely speak languages other than English at home and large numbers follow a religion quite different from Christianity. What are the implications for Australian Christians? Using our 'changing lanes' analogy, drivers find themselves sharing the road with such vehicles as cars, trucks, buses, bicycles, motorcycles and caravans. Good drivers adjust their driving practices accordingly, so that traffic can flow smoothly and safely. Similarly, churches ministering across cultures make necessary adjustments to cater for the different ethnicities and cultures of people with whom they are mixing. You probably know plenty of Christians in Australia who largely ignore this situation, and continue to attend churches that are predominantly composed of people who share the same or similar ethnic backgrounds, whether Anglo, Korean, Chinese, Samoan, etc. Let's face it, it's usually much easier to associate with people who are like us — same cultural background, same language, with similar likes and dislikes when it comes to food, pastimes, worship style, etc.

It is not wrong to relate with and minister to people with whom we feel a strong affinity. Indeed, we should make the most of the opportunities such commonalities provide. However, we've seen in Module 1 that God wants to see all people provided with the opportunity to know him and find salvation, regardless of their ethnic or cultural background. The more our hearts become attuned to God's heart, the more we will be moved to cross cultural barriers and relate deeply with people who differ from us in many ways. If we were to follow our natural instincts, to merely swim with the current, as it were, then we would have little to do with such people and confine ourselves to superficial interactions. But the Lord calls his people to be counter-cultural — to swim against the current — and he can equip and empower us to do just that.

A church in Sydney's west was once almost entirely Anglo Aussie in composition. Then migrants steadily flowed into the suburbs surrounding the church. The leaders and a small group of the congregation realised that this was not happening by chance. They saw new residents with many needs, including the need to know and follow *(cont.)*

Swimming against the current

Jesus. They implemented some changes. They visited the homes of local recently-arrived settlers. They enlisted the help of experienced cross-cultural workers to train the congregation. They made the church services more accessible to people from non-English speaking backgrounds. Some disgruntled congregation members moved to other churches. Those who stayed embraced the changes to varying degrees, and soon came up against some jarring cross-cultural experiences. There were different ideas about time, style of worship, role of leadership, and the nature of hospitality. Some members came to realise how racist and intolerant they were, deep down. But they persevered, and members whom the authors interviewed say it really has been worth it. In the process everyone has learnt from cultures other than the one they are comfortable with. This church speaks loudly to the surrounding, very multi-ethnic neighbourhood. People from around 40 ethnic backgrounds and 30 different language groups have come through the door. Many have stayed, including some from non-Christian backgrounds.

2.3 Biblical reflection

1. Identify and discuss incidents that occurred during Jesus' ministry which show him to be the Saviour for all people whatever their ethnic identity (e.g. John 4:39-42).

2. Identify and discuss sayings of Jesus that concern the salvation of non-Jewish people (e.g. Matthew 8:11-12).

3. Identify teachings of Jesus that lay the foundation for an understanding of God's people as not defined by Jewish ethnic identity (e.g. Matthew 15:16-19; compare verses 1-11).

Until the last quarter of the last century, a certain church in Melbourne's inner east was a reasonably busy middle-class church. Around 70-120 mainly Anglo Aussie members, who lived nearby, attended each Sunday. But the demographic mix of the region changed through immigration. This was followed by a movement of longer-term residents to other suburbs. The mostly older congregation members could see little need to relate to minority groups in the community. They were seen as being too different, having their own faiths and languages, or maybe just too hard to include. And the pastor had little experience in cross-cultural ministry. As the congregation aged and many Aussies moved to 'whiter' suburbs, the church shrank to the point where the denomination's leaders decided it was no longer viable.

2.4 Contrasting responses

Sadly, the story above can be repeated around Australia. Churches like these become irrelevant to their own communities, and some of the members appear to prefer 'their' church to die rather than to change. Statistics related to church closures around Australia are difficult to obtain, but it's obvious that many have shut down, or amalgamated with other nearby congregations.

As you can see from these two short case studies (and you may know many churches that lie somewhere between these two examples), Australia's multi-ethnic nature has clear implications for the church. The fact that you're reading this book and perhaps studying it in a group reflects the fact that you can see what's happening, and would like to be proactive rather than waiting till it's almost too late.

2.5 A multi-ethnic church?

The authors often hear friends say that their church is very multi-ethnic. What that sometimes means is that the people themselves are from a range of ethnic backgrounds. However, services start and finish on time, have a song-sermon-prayers-song style format, and are conducted entirely in English. That is, the style and emphasis often do not reflect the wide range of ethnicities in attendance, and neither does the leadership. They reflect the make-up and preferences of the majority, or dominant group in the congregation, which in many mainstream churches will usually be the Anglo Aussies. Maybe that's why you're reading and/or studying this book — your church is like this, and you'd like to see it be more multi-ethnic, a community in which people from a wide range of ethnic backgrounds feel that they are welcome, and are full, participating members. When that doesn't happen, those from minority ethnic groupings often move on, or try to set up own-language/own-ethnicity congregations, or join existing own-language churches, with only limited links to the wider Australian church.

2.6 Ethnic diversity/identity

A church in NSW had an influx of East Africans over a period in the late 1990's. These people were welcomed by the mainly Anglo Aussie congregation but, with a few exceptions, congregation members struggled to understand their culture or preferred ways of worshiping, and few members tried to learn their names. The busy pastor didn't realise how much their community leaders would appreciate a regular visit from the pastor. After a while, numbers of these re-settlers began to slip away. Some joined other churches, and some stopped attending church altogether.

Make no mistake, ethnic diversity is a complex subject, but a fascinating one with which Australian Christians need to grapple if we are to be servants of Jesus who share him in relevant ways with our increasingly diverse group of neighbours, friends and work colleagues.

Newer arrivals may look different from the majority population, but they may not all be at the same level of 'newness' as one another. Perhaps Figure 1 will help you understand more about this diversity and its implications for cross-cultural ministry initiatives.

Figure 1: Ethnic Diversity Continuum

Figure 1 above identifies seven broad ways in which people's ethnic identity is expressed in Australia. The arrows point in both directions, indicating that many people do not retain the same ethnic identity for the entirety of their lives or even have the same ethnic identity in all social contexts. Some people, for example, begin their lives in Australia as those who strongly identify with their culture of origin. But as time goes by they move more towards the right of the continuum, as they adapt and adjust to mainstream Australian culture in its various expressions. By contrast, others begin life as those who strongly identify with Australian mainstream culture but who later seek to rediscover the culture of their parents and grandparents.

Let's take a closer look at the different ways in which ethnic identity is expressed, remembering that it is not to be confused with some concept of 'race', but is a product of combining together such things as language, culture, religion, and ancestral roots.

On the far left of the spectrum, **Group A** are people who immigrated to

Australia or were born here, yet they tend to be isolated in a cultural setting that separates them from the majority of the Australian population and from mainstream Australian culture with its major subcultures. One example might be elderly Burmese refugees who re-settled in Australia in the past 5-10 years, and never managed to pick up much English. They tend to congregate only with fellow Burmese. By contrast, their children and grandchildren typically will identify much more strongly with Australian mainstream culture. So Group A migrants depend heavily on their children when they are not sure how to respond to the unavoidable demands and issues that Australian society presents.

> Comments by a South Sudanese migrant to Blacktown, Sydney:
>
> "There are situations where children bring notes home from school and parents are unable to read them. Children learn language fast and don't have trouble making friends." Edward Massimino, Sudanese refugee. (NSW Migration Heritage Centre, 2011).

Identifying a little more with mainstream Australian culture are those who make up **Group B**. Like those in Group A they also identify themselves with a language-culture group. They immigrated to Australia and they are Australian citizens, but they often refer to their country of origin as 'home', idealising their own culture and using it to judge Australian culture. They tend to hang on tenaciously to a language other than English. An example might be the so-called 'astronauts' who were born in Hong Kong, live in Australia, but travel back and forth for work or to connect with relatives.

Group C is composed of second generation Aussies. They identify with their parents' culture, but were either born and grew up in Australia or came here at an early age. They are bi-lingual and bi-cultural, and often have two worlds at the core of their being. Their own parents don't always understand them. An example might be the Australian-born 50 year-old offspring of migrants from Greece living in Melbourne. It is especially second generation youth who confirm the findings of much contemporary research that there is no such thing as a fixed ethnic identity. Such young people often have multiple identities that they adopt in differing contexts. For further discussion of issues related to second generation people and their relationship to their parents' churches, see Appendix D.

> "Young people are the ideal bridge in most communities, especially in immigrant communities, because they are raised in traditional ways but schooled in the ways of the dominant culture. Young people typically accompany their parents to the clinic, school, faith institution, and many other places. Sometimes, they translate for their non-English speaking parents. Therefore, they are likely to know where their parents go for help and who organizes the events in their community." (KU Work Group for Community Health and Development 2015).

Traditional v Trendy

People in **Group D** identify with a language/culture group when it's convenient and beneficial. Most have only a limited understanding of a language other than English. An example might be the descendants of the German Lutherans who came to South Australia in the 1830's to escape persecution. They are culturally aware, and some continue to celebrate their German festivals.

People in **Group E** are those whose appearance identifies them as being not part of the majority population, but their relationship with their ethnic heritages and languages is close to nonexistent. They may or may not be assimilated into the majority culture. Some if not many non-Chinese speaking Australian-born Chinese people may fall into this zone in the spectrum.

People in **Group F** are those who have moved out of their culture of origin and have been effectively assimilated into majority Australian culture. They may or may not have been born in Australia, they routinely speak English and have more or less adopted an Aussie lifestyle.

And finally, ethnic minority people in **Group G** are those who not only totally identify themselves with mainstream Australian culture but are readily recognised as Australians by others. At this point in Australia's migration history, the appearance of such people will enable them to be recognised by others as representative of majority culture. The time of the White Australia policy is fading further and further into the past, and with it there has been a fading of 'whiteness' as the identifying characteristic of those thought of as representative of the majority population. So quickly is the ethnic face of Australia changing that it will not be long before Groups F and G merge. As things stand, an example of Group G might be a young banker whose grandparents migrated to Australia from Italy in the first half of the 20th century and who has a complexion more consistent with that of many who live in Southern Europe rather than in Northern Europe.

As we have already emphasised, these categories are dynamic, not static. People are complex. Cultural drift is a common phenomenon, with people moving between categories, sometimes returning, for example, to their cultural roots, sometimes moving further away from them. Someone else has talked of 'layers of identity', with all of us switching between them.

> A Malaysian friend who migrated to Australia more than 25 years ago to study and work acknowledges that he does not feel fully acculturated to Australia, but that he tries to take the best from both cultures, and to avoid the worst.

Understanding these different expressions of ethnic identity has important implications for Christian ministry across cultures. How we view others does not necessarily accord with how people view themselves. For example, there are young second or third generation Australians whom those in mainline denominational churches may view as being very Aussie, but whom they are unlikely to reach. Targeted ministries like that established and led by Ray Galea (a second generation Maltese now at St. Alban's MBM [Multicultural Bible Ministry] in Rooty Hill, Sydney), have been particularly effective in drawing together a wide range of such Australians. Alternatively, there are many first generation migrants who value being able to worship in their heart language and in cultural forms with which they are familiar. This does not mean that churches should not reach out to first generation migrants, but they may need to be creative in providing contexts that are sensitive to the linguistic and cultural needs of such folk.

For many migrants, ethnic identity is very much bound up with religious identity. It is still largely the case, for example, that to be Greek is to be Greek Orthodox. For those who have grown up as Hindus or Muslims, being a Hindu or Muslim is an inextricable part of their identity. They will, however, vary in the extent to which they identify with their national culture and mainstream Australian culture. This has important implications for those seeking to minister amongst the different migrant groups.

2.7 Summary

By now, you're aware that the coming of people from many of the nations of the world to Australia is inevitable and will continue to gather momentum. Many Christians and churches are responding to the Biblical command to welcome, embrace and share the good news of Jesus with everyone. Some are not. Multi-ethnicity is multi-faceted, with some challenging implications for Christians and churches. But learning about, and trying to grasp, what's at work in the lives and cultures of those we hope to befriend is a very good starting place as we relate sensitively and try to serve Jesus in our relationships with them.

In the next module we'll consider some of the hindrances to effective outreach, and how they might be overcome.

2.8 Questions

1. What are the important lessons you can learn from churches that are reaching out effectively across cultures? In what ways is your church already effective cross-culturally?

2. What are some of the pitfalls you should try to avoid? Do you think your church has already made some of these mistakes?

3. Do you feel that your church members understand ethnic diversity and its implications? If not, what can you do to help that situation?

4. What are the implications of the Ethnic Diversity Continuum model (Figure 1) for how we 'do' church?

5. To what extent is it possible for any particular church to reach everyone within its orbit?

Notes

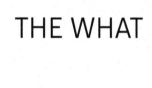

THE WHAT

Module 3

**CHANGING ROAD RESPONSES: DEALING WITH
HINDRANCES TO MINISTRY ACROSS CULTURES**

3.1 Prayer

3.2 Introduction

When driving, we often encounter potholes, detours, road closures and the like. In some places, thick fog or ice can make driving hazardous. And in working across cultures, there can be a number of hindrances to ministry. This module examines some of those and explores ways to deal with them.

3.3 Biblical reflection

Read Acts 10.
Note especially verses 27-28 (compare verses 14-15), 34-35, 47-48.

1. What does this incident reveal about obstacles that stood in the way of Jewish Christian outreach to non-Jewish people?

2. What obstacles to ministering across cultures stand in our own way?

Daunting task

3.4 Common hindrances in cross-cultural ministry

In Matthew's Great Commission, Jesus commanded his disciples to bring all peoples on the face of the globe under his Lordship. This is a task way beyond the capacity of any individual Christian or of any particular local church or Christian organisation. There are legitimate limits to what any believer, church or Christian organisation can contribute towards the accomplishment of this immense task. Not that we must limit God; he often uses his people to do far more than anything they would ever have dared to think possible. In prayer we constantly look to God to do things that are beyond our limits.

But in addition to such legitimate limits there are other factors that stand in the way of doing what the Lord would have us do. Obedience to him will move us to find ways of overcoming such obstacles to realising the Lord's will.

A. Reasons and excuses

"It's not a priority for us!" "It will bring conflict into the church!" "We already have too much on our plate!" "We don't have the resources!" "We've had no training!" "We don't speak their language!" "We already have a strong ministry within our own language group that we need to maintain!" These are some of the responses we can expect to receive when we challenge churches to reach out to those who don't correspond to the ethnic and cultural makeup of those who currently constitute their church community. Sometimes such factors may be valid reasons why a church should focus its efforts, but sometimes they are rationalisations for our failure to hear and obey our Lord. The distinction between reasons and excuses is not always easy to determine, as situations can vary considerably. But we can say that a church that is not seeking the Lord's will through concerted prayer is not in a good position to tell the difference.

B. Legitimate limits

When it comes to reaching ethnic minorities living in Australia, there are many legitimate limits faced by individuals, churches and Christian organisations. In this huge continent, location will often place limits. Inability to speak the language of certain migrants will present obvious limitations, though some strategies such as ESL (English as a Second Language) ministries may enjoy some measure of success in reducing such limits. The financial capacity and size of a church may pose limits. For example, a large Cantonese-speaking Chinese church may well find it has the capacity to initiate a Mandarin-speaking ministry for migrants coming from mainland China. But this may be beyond the capacity of a small Cantonese-speaking church.

However, with the help of God, we can go some way to addressing and overcoming even legitimate limits.

C. Illegitimate hindrances

i. No burden for the lost

An obvious obstruction standing in the way of seeking to reach ethnic minorities with the gospel is a failure to see and treat those outside of Christ as lost. Many churches, whatever their ethnic composition, are not seriously engaged in evangelising any outsiders, not even those like themselves, let alone those who come from different linguistic, ethnic and cultural sectors of society.

ii. Over-dependence on social factors and feeling comfortable within one's own people group

Some think that reaching Vietnamese people should be left to Vietnamese churches, reaching Sudanese people should be left to Sudanese churches, reaching Arabic-speaking people should be left to Arabic-speaking churches, and so on. But reaching people from a particular linguistic, ethnic or cultural background is not a simple matter of leaving this to churches composed of like people. Many churches are effective in reaching people from their own range of ethnicity to only a limited degree. For example, some churches are formed to meet the needs of inter-related families. Indeed, there is a very real danger that church life will be shaped more by sociological factors than the demands of the gospel. The reality is that some churches operate more like culture clubs. Such churches may feel no need to recruit members. Because these churches are made up of Christians who belong to minorities, it is natural for some migrants to come to these churches because they are places where they meet and form relationships with others who speak the same language and with whom they have much more in common than with majority culture Australians. As a consequence, many of these churches do not expend any special effort to reach out to outsiders. Yet these outsiders include many who do in fact speak the same language and whose ethnic and cultural background is not significantly different from that of those in the church.

iii. Ethnic difference

Often, language churches do not attract people from certain ethnic groups even when they do speak the same language and share many cultural traits. Ethnicity is often a divider. The members of most Indonesian churches in Australia are largely of Chinese ethnicity. Karen and Karenni Burmese normally form their own churches that largely exclude other Burmese. Sometimes, such gathering around ethnic identity is merely a case of "birds of a feather flock together." Unfortunately, however, it is sometimes also accompanied by an attitude that says to others, "You are not one of us. You are not welcome."

iv. Ethnocentrism and racism

> " The person who has not visited another village will think only his mother's cooking is sweet."
> WEST AFRICAN PROVERB

Ethnocentrism, the tendency to consider our own cultural heritage superior to all others, is pretty much a universal phenomenon. Pride in one's own culture, however, does not necessarily involve a spirit of rejection of other cultures. But when this is added to other factors such as fear of 'the other' and the unknown, it is not difficult to see how people can often be racist in their attitudes (prejudice) and behaviour (discrimination). "I am not racist BUT..." The word 'but' is the give-away here. Any church that is serious about reaching ethnic minorities must be helped, in a wise and appropriate manner, to deal with early racism and attitudes that are inconsistent with the generous gospel heart that results from deeply appreciating the grace and love of God.

v. Painful history

We must not be trite when we speak of the need to profoundly absorb the reality of God's grace. Somewhat understandably, for example, centuries of oppression and humiliation as non-Muslim minorities under Muslim rule have made it particularly difficult for many Arabic-speaking Christians to reach out to Muslims who speak the same language and share many cultural characteristics.

vi. Lack of gospel-driven leadership

❝❝ Neither be idle in the means, nor make an idol of the means."
WILLIAM SECKER
17TH CENTURY ENGLISH CLERGYMAN

A lack of gospel-driven leadership adds yet further height to obstacles that are already difficult to hurdle. Leaders often feel pressured to do only what they feel they can do well so that they can be seen to be successful in their ministries. This may well deter them from engaging in ministry across cultures.

Gospel-driven leadership seeks to equip the saints for works of ministry (Ephesians 4:12). If there are high levels of apathy in a church then this may be due to the failure of leaders to involve people in ministry. Many church leaders feel that they are expected to exercise many of the spiritual gifts themselves, and it is often the case that the gifts of church members are poorly and inadequately tapped and brought into service.

In many Australian churches where the main language used is not English, a missionary mindset is needed by first generation leaders and members in relating and ministering to their English-speaking second generation members and vice-versa. Such is the starkness of the difference in culture between the generations. One Korean church in Sydney, blessed with visionary leadership, has recognised this reality and has run workshops in the church to address these cultural differences. In many Korean churches there is a 'silent exodus', with high percentages of young people leaving the church of their parents and often church altogether after leaving school. In contrast, this Korean church has an extraordinarily high retention rate. It attributes this especially *(cont.)*

> to the deliberate way in which it has trained its high schoolers to lead
> Bible study groups for young people.

vii. Preserving church culture

Whether intended or not, it is often the case that when church members
do seek to engage with outsiders they are operating on the model of 'come
to us on our terms' rather than 'go to them on their terms'. This is another
way of saying that our own religious culture has become so important to us
that it trumps the gospel. In both majority and minority culture churches,
such issues as music preference, dress code and liturgy can stand in the way
of fruitful gospel ministry. The philosopher John Stuart Mill (1806-1873)
once declared, "The despotism of custom is everywhere the standing hindrance to human advancement." It is certainly true that church culture is
often a major hindrance to the advancement of the gospel. Many Christians
lack the cultural intelligence and competence needed to negotiate cultural
differences. Further, by its very nature, culture exists to serve the needs of
those who belong to that culture. The more dependent we are on preserv-
ing our own religious culture the more preoccupied we will be with meeting our own needs. The needs of outsiders are then inevitably neglected. A
healthy church will be characterised by a strong inner life and, as Acts 2:42-
47 illustrates, this is integral to a church's drawing power. However, when
culture rather than the gospel is the primary shaper of church life, then we
have an unhealthy church that often repels rather than attracts outsiders.

viii. Confusion of gospel and culture

The reality is that everybody is immersed in culture, whatever form it may
assume and no matter how distasteful it may be to those for whom that
culture is alien. Culture is inescapable and it is a reality we must treat very
seriously. Another obstacle is erected from our side when, in addition to
presenting the claims of Christ as Lord, we require people to jump through
our cultural hoops as well. We often present the gospel in terms that ob-
scure it beneath layers of our own cultural understanding and values. Over-

coming barriers to cross-cultural communication must begin with a clear understanding of the essential nature of the gospel itself, clearly distinguishing it from its cultural attendants. However, insensitivity to the cultural beliefs, values and social structures of those to whom one is ministering also places a roadblock in the path of the gospel. Indian evangelist, R.K. Murthi, once said, "Do not bring us the Gospel as a potted plant. Bring us the seed of the Gospel and plant it in our soil." People will reject the gospel because they don't believe it is true. But we don't want them to spurn it because it is falsely deemed to be Western or foreign. Suppose your church has the potential to reach out to Vietnamese Buddhists. If you simply depend on your present church services being able to attract and hold such people, you will probably be disappointed. You may well need to establish a distinct ministry to Vietnamese that expresses sensitivity to their cultural needs. This does not mean that such a ministry cannot be made a vital part of your church community, but it does mean you need to be careful not to adopt culturally insensitive approaches to reaching Buddhists.

> A suburban Anglican church encountered two difficulties in seeking to develop a ministry to first generation Vietnamese refugees. Firstly, the tradition of having attendees kneel at the communion rail was offensive to some refugees, recalling painful memories of being forced by Viet Cong to kneel in fear. Secondly, many Vietnamese, when they attended the main service, were shocked and offended to see the young pastor leading the service while wearing a pair of shorts.

ix. Cultural barriers

There are always those migrants who want to integrate or assimilate into mainstream culture and who may even be attracted by the cultural differences they experience in this strange church setting. But many others will remain unreached unless we are prepared to go to them on their terms. Such an approach to ministry may necessitate the launching of new ministries outside the normal structures of church life. For example, there are religious conservatives who may be driven further away from rather than nearer to Jesus if we were to bring them to a church service in which they see what they may regard as improper relations between males and females, inappropriate female dress and a lack of reverence for holy books.

x. Cultural distance

This highlights afresh that one of the most fundamental principles of any effective cross-cultural ministry is that of reducing cultural distance if we can. For a church that is serious about reaching people from ethnic minorities, this requires giving thought not merely to the methods and structures of ministry. Some churches flounder because they choose the wrong person or persons to spearhead a ministry. It will not do merely to appoint a leader who is of the same ethnicity and able to speak the same language to reach people from particular ethnic backgrounds. Notwithstanding such advantages, other factors, whether personal or sociological, may make this person a poor fit for the people the church is seeking to reach.

xi. Lack of community

Western individualism does not fit well with placing a high value on community. Jesus commands us, "Love one another. As I have loved you, so you must love one another. By this everyone will know that you are my disciples, if you love one another." (John 13:34-35). Einstein thought Buddhism would make a good cosmic religion because he saw in it a meaningful unity. Buddhists often stress peace and harmony. Trying to point out cracks in the Buddhist façade misses the point. When Buddhists see fighting and division in our churches this sets up a formidable barrier to belief. To them, this means that Christianity is not a religion that brings peace and harmony. Quite apart from obvious disunity in our churches, many who come from Asian and other backgrounds would find very little warmth, hospitality and family-feeling in the way activities are run, and in the socialising afterwards.

xii. Spiritual opposition

In his book *Powers of Darkness*, Clinton Arnold (1992, p. 148) rightly observes: "Even in Christian ministry the spiritual dimension is often ignored.

Ineffective evangelism, for example, is often attributed to a lack of training or persuasive skill rather than powerful demonic hindrance." Paul reminds us: "…our struggle is not against flesh and blood, but against the rulers, against the authorities, against the powers of this dark world, and against the spiritual forces of evil in the heavenly realms" (Ephesians 6:12). Impediments to effective gospel ministry, whether to those who share our own culture and ethnic identity or not, are part and parcel of spiritual warfare.

D. Encouragement from the Book of Acts

The early church as depicted in the book of Acts was not introspective. Further, it was a dynamic and united body of believers strongly led by visionary leaders passionate about communicating the gospel of the resurrection. But it is worth remembering that it began as an exclusively Jewish church.

The narrative of Acts 10 graphically describes Peter's feelings of revulsion when asked to eat the unclean food God served up for him on the tablecloth that descended from heaven in Peter's vision. In context, this mirrored the revulsion he normally would have felt if asked to enter the home of a Gentile or to eat with Gentiles. If things had been left to run along the normal railway tracks then the gospel train would never have left Jewish Christian territory. This would have been so despite the undoubted commitment of the apostles to proclaiming the gospel of the resurrection even in the face of persecution and suffering. The fact is that gospel ministry left to itself always travels a short cultural distance. Even in the early church, believers naturally communicated the gospel to people like themselves. It takes a special work of God and deliberate decision and action if gospel ministry is to have a significant impact on people unlike ourselves. Churches that are to be effective in reaching the ethnic minorities of Australia must be open to God's special leading and be highly intentional.

One of the authors was invited by a suburban denominational church to help it to reach out across cultures. The ethnic composition of the community around the church was composed of many from Chinese (*cont.*)

and Korean backgrounds. Leaders clearly communicated to the church community that the author had been asked to help the church in this way. Over a three-month period, the leaders arranged for meetings with home groups and other key ministry groups in the church, in addition to planned sermons and communications during church services, to prepare church members for the cultural differences they would experience. A pastor of Chinese ethnicity was added to the ministry team. The church today is very different from the substantially Anglo Aussie church it once was.

In 1 Corinthians 9:12 Paul says, "...we put up with anything rather than hinder the gospel of Christ." The word 'hinder' has a meaning that arose out of its military use. During a retreat, the road might be cut into or broken up to delay and hinder the pursuing enemy. Paul is determined that nothing should delay or prevent the progress of the gospel. He is determined to ensure that he does not act in a way that results in a roadblock or obstacle being placed in the path of the gospel. Are we? In the next section we explore how these hindrances might be overcome.

3.5 Overcoming hindrances in cross-cultural ministry

Perhaps you can see in yourself and your church some of those very hindrances we've been discussing and wonder what can be done about them. Or you can see inertia — or outright resistance — in your church to the idea of reaching out in love to the nations in our towns and cities with a longing to see them also included in the family of the living God as our brothers and sisters in Christ. Be encouraged! God is well able to address this. Many churches around Australia have in fact changed in their outlook and focus and have removed or surmounted barriers. Some are now seeing reflected in their own church life something of the rich diversity that God has brought about in their neighbourhoods. Others have contributed in different ways to the ministry of the gospel among people from different ethnic and cultural backgrounds.

The section above has pointed out some of the challenging obstacles to churches reaching out across cultures. They can be numerous and engender strong resistance to change. But don't be discouraged. The section finished on an encouraging note by reminding us that, though the early church was exclusively Jewish, God worked in the lives of some of its leaders, showing them that he intends for all the nations to be incorporated into the community of salvation. In the early church a most wonderful thing happened — Jews and Gentiles began worshiping together. Let's expect God to do amazing things in our churches, too.

A. Helpful approaches to overcoming hindrances

i. Pray for transformation

" The little estimate we put on prayer is evidence from the little time we give to it." (Bounds 1962, p.12).

E.M. BOUNDS (1835-1913)
AMERICAN CHRISTIAN AUTHOR

As with all areas of life, we need to ask God to search our hearts and thoughts for ungodly attitudes and practices (Psalms 139:23-24) and to transform our minds when it comes to people in our locality and churches who are unlike us (Romans 12:2). We need not only to pray for this to happen, but be willing to allow God to change us.

In 2008 John Fry received a Medal of the Order of Australia (OAM) for his service to the community through church organisations, and social justice initiatives to assist prisoners and detainees. Yet, only seven years previously, in June 2001, John was reflecting on the Apostle Peter's visit to Cornelius. He felt the Lord was rebuking him for his own attitude to new arrivals in Australia. He says humbly, "I was covertly racist, as a product of my upbringing and I was disturbed by my attitude." Two months later he spoke about being "absolutely shocked and appalled by (the Tampa crisis)." He decided to do something about it. Two days later he was visiting refugees at the Villawood Detention Centre. *(cont.)*

John went on to establish *Neighbours and Friends,* a very helpful ministry that enlists Aussie Christians to befriend and assist refugees and migrants, and to treat them as who they should be – neighbours and friends (Percy 2008).

It is not merely the attitudes of individual Christians that need to change. We need change, often substantial change, in our churches if they are to be effective in drawing people to Christ. Are we expecting our minority-background friends and associates to effortlessly fit in with the ways we meet and worship? Have we set up cultural barriers, often unconsciously, which we expect newcomers to overcome if they are to be welcomed and loved in our communities, homes and churches? It is just these kinds of questions that we need to ask ourselves, as we look to God to address attitudes and practices that are ungodly and unhelpful.

Many Australian denominational churches have not been successful in attracting the so-called 'working class'. It is arguable that they would have been far more successful in doing this had they recognised the extent to which migrants have made up this significant segment of the Australian population. Churches have often failed to discriminate between gospel and culture. This, together with an unpreparedness to change or modify aspects of church culture, has conspired to alienate or discourage outsiders — often migrants and, therefore, often the 'working class'.

In his 2004 Presidential Address, Peter Jensen, then the Anglican Archbishop of Sydney, reflected on how British Australia had been profoundly changed by migrants from Europe and Asia. He asked: "Has our church assimilated this migrant flow and allowed itself to be changed by it?" Significantly, he linked this with the commonly recognised inability of churches to reach the so-called 'working class': "What we failed to see was that the post-war working class was going to be dominated by migrants; newcomers like my taxi driver, rich in determination, and even in education, but poorer in communication skills if the language had to be English; poor especially in an understanding of how their *(cont.)*

new homeland 'worked'; fearful of losing their children to its very different ways." (Jensen 2004).

Similarly, in his book *Seeds Blowing in the Wind*, Jim Houston remarked: "Another valid way of viewing our relative non-involvement with migrants is to see it as a subset of our traditional non-involvement with the urban working class." (1994, p. 11).

ii. The need for focused ministries

One of the keys to overcoming the hurdles to successful ministry across cultures is the development of ministry initiatives that are directed at reaching a particular section of the community. This is demonstrated in the following case study.

Ray Galea, founding pastor of Multicultural Bible Ministries (MBM), Rooty Hill, Sydney, is of Maltese ethnic extraction. His church runs an annual 'Wogs for Christ' conference. Ray describes himself as a 'wog' and his church as targeting 'second generation wogs', as exemplified by the story of Sarkis who is part-Armenian and part-Assyrian. Sarkis had attended MBM but later joined another church closer to his home. However, two years later he was back at MBM. He was positive about the other church but said to Ray, "I feel like you understand me." As Ray remarks, "What he meant was that we have a lot more shared assumptions. There were the silly things, like growing up in homes that has plastic on the carpet, and there were the big things of living in two cultures." Sarkis' English was excellent, so language was not the barrier. He simply felt more connected with MBM because they were to his mind 'wogs' like him. As a more mature Christian now, Sarkis would probably not feel this need as strongly as he did at that time. But Ray makes the point that "it's easy to overlook the real differences of second generation ethnics and simply assume they would (or should) naturally fit in to an Aussie-dominated church. Most need a ministry that allows them less hurdles to hear the gospel. What we need are more second generation, wog-friendly churches." (Galea 2004).

iii. Don't give up!

The issues we've been considering in this module might sound daunting, or produce feelings of inadequacy in you, especially if your cross-cultural experience to date has been limited. Perhaps this is a helpful starting point as you admit your inadequacy before God and call on his help. He speaks all languages and understands all cultures. Plenty of Christians have undertaken what you are trying to do, in God's strength, and have survived and been effective in outreach. Try to persevere; you will probably make many mistakes, but the authors have found that people of other backgrounds will often see if we care about them.

iv. Include your pastor(s) and leaders

It's vital that your pastor and church leaders be included in the self-examination, prayer, education and skills acquisition outlined in Module 4. The authors have seen plenty of examples of churches where one or two congregation members are passionate about the church reaching out cross-culturally, but where little lasting progress occurred, partly because the leadership merely sanctioned it or welcomed it, but didn't get personally involved. Module 5 picks up this important area in more detail.

> One impediment is letting cross-cultural ministry be the pet project of just a few people in the church. A large suburban church decided to develop a multi-ethnic English-speaking ministry which took off for a while and then flagged somewhat. A friend took over the leadership of this ministry and at the same time as they were trying to give it a fresh boost, the church decided to embark on a church plant. There was one key reason why the multi-ethnic ministry continued to be held back: it was because the leaders of the church did not treat it as being as important as other ministries in which they themselves were much more directly involved, such as the church plant. The church plant was constantly prayed for in church services, regularly featured in church bulletins and other publications i.e. given a high profile. By contrast, while the leaders verbally expressed positive support for the clearly highly strategic multi-ethnic ministry, it was not given a similarly high profile.

B. Particular hindrances to ministry across cultures and possible solutions

 A problem well stated is a problem half solved."

CHARLES F. KETTERING (1876-1958)

AMERICAN INVENTOR

Table 1: Development of any form of God-honouring gospel ministry

Hindrance	Possible solutions
Absence of love and unity. (John 13:34-35)	Spiritual revitalisation (prayer, ministry of word, etc.). Practical helps: a. Attend Peacewise seminars (www. peacewise.org.au). b. Study Harry Reeder, *From Embers to a Flame. How God can Revitalize your Church (2008)*. c. Arrange for a church consultancy.

Table 2: Development of God-honouring multi-ethnic ministry

Hindrance	Possible Solutions

Racism and ethnocentrism.	1. Hold workshops.
	 2. Exposure to people from other cultures:
	    a. Getting them to give testimonies in church.
	    b. Having church members minister in a different cultural context (e.g. short-term mission trip either overseas or within Australia).

Feeling that it's not a priority for us.	1. Demographic research and analysis. 2. Address this through Bible study. 3. Address this through your preaching program.

Hindrance	Possible solutions
Cont.	4. Explore the importance of ministry across cultures in the light of your church's mission, vision and core values.
Fear of the unknown – will I be able to do it?	1. Talk to people who have already done it. 2. Get training. 3. Start with a modest venture.
Feeling that it will bring conflict and disruption into the church.	1. If your church doesn't have conflict it's probably dead! 2. Learn how to handle conflict from those already engaged in ministry across cultures. 3. Arrange for Peacewise training (www.peacewise.org.au). 4. Prepare the congregation well beforehand. 5. ESL classes are a great place for people to meet across cultures. 6. Develop a change management program.
Believing that we already have a flourishing ministry, so we'll concentrate on that.	If there are already vigorous evangelical ministries to people from other cultures in your area then you MAY be right to do this. HOWEVER: 1. If not, these people need to hear the gospel. 2. The churches best situated to reach out to people across cultures are those that already have the resources (property, people and finances) to do this. 3. It is much more difficult for churches in serious decline to do this.

(Cont.)

Hindrance	Possible solutions
The pastor feeling, "I have too much on my plate already. I have no energy to get something else going."	1. In the very near future set aside a day or weekend for prayer, lay it all before the Lord and seek his direction and help.
	2. Spend extended time discussing your situation with a ministry consultant and/or with a friend or friends who will give you sharp and helpful insights.
	3. To avoid a recurrence of this you need to lead yourself and your church through a thorough planning process.
	4. While your backing will be crucial to any new ministry don't think and act as though its total success depends on you. Give primary responsibility for multi-ethnic ministry to a team, but do not use your busyness and tiredness as an excuse for distancing yourself from this ministry.
Having a very few members with the gifts to spearhead ministry across cultures and those who have them are already fully committed to other ministries.	1. Develop a sister-church relationship with a resource-rich church and seek to address this issue together.
	2. Develop a ministry across cultures that involves cooperation with other churches.
	3. Look for suitable workers from the focus group you are seeking to reach who would be willing to join your church and become part of your ministry team. This might include keeping an eye out for students about to graduate from a Bible college.
	4. Personally approach some church members who are not already over-committed, explain how vital cross-cultural ministry is, and help them to see how they could make a good contribution.

Hindrance	Possible solutions
The pastor feeling pressured to run a 'successful' ministry and feeling he needs to emphasise the ministries he knows he can do well.	1. In the very near future set aside a day or weekend for prayer, lay it all before the Lord and seek his direction and help. To whom does he want you to reach out? 2. Spend extended time discussing your situation with a ministry consultant and/or with a friend or friends who will give you sharp and helpful insights. 3. You need to lead yourself and your church through a thorough planning process and, as part of this, identify your core values (will 'success' be one of them?). 4. Don't think and act as though all ministries are dependent on your gifting and know-how — the Lord gives other Christians gifts as well! If you feel out of your depth, look for others to whom you can give primary responsibility for ministry across cultures. 5. Form a team, but do not use your lack of confidence as an excuse for distancing yourself from this ministry. 6. There is nothing wrong with learning something new and making mistakes in the process.
Not speaking 'their' language.	1. Add someone to your ministry team who does speak their language. 2. Locate and make available acceptable Christian resources (tracts, books, videos, cassettes) in their language. 3. Develop an ESL (English as a Second Language) ministry or run Easy English Bible studies and have an Easy English church service.

(Cont.)

Hindrance	Possible solutions
Difficulty in locating acceptable Christian resources in the target language.	1. Contact people who are engaged in ministry to this people group. Often resources are already being used, but have not been professionally published and made widely available. Don't limit your search for such resources — use the internet also to find resources being used overseas. 2. Take less than adequate resources as a starting point and revamp and improve them (being mindful of copyright issues). 3. Start with an appropriate English language resource and get a native speaker to help you translate it into the other language and help you to make any necessary adjustments for cultural reasons.
Individuals feeling unsure or ignorant about how best to go about initiating contact and carrying out a conversation with others from a different culture.	1. Study a book on cross-cultural communication. 2. Attend workshops on cross-cultural communication. 3. Practise in the neighbourhood. 4. Ask insiders from other cultures to teach you about their cultures.

3.6 Summary

There are many reasons for the lack of appropriate responses by Christians and churches toward new settlers in Australia. Some of the reasons are legitimate, many are not. The proposed solutions for overcoming the hindrances discussed above have been adopted by churches that have a vision to embrace other cultures, with encouraging results. However, the implementation of some of these solutions will also require us to be culturally intelligent. Increasing our cultural intelligence will remove many obstacles — we will focus on this in the next module.

3.7 Questions

1. As you think about ministry to ethnic minorities, what do you see as legitimate limits in your own church or ministry context? What are the illegitimate hindrances?

2. Which of the hindrances you have identified poses the biggest problem in your ministry context? Analyse this hindrance and identify the factors that explain why it is so significant.

3. How can church members who are used to a long-established model of church be helped to see the need of the church to develop other models in order to reach out to people from other cultural backgrounds?

4. How can already stretched pastors and other leaders be best resourced and helped to provide leadership for developing ministry across cultures?

5. How can church members be helped to understand people of other cultures so as to avoid hurtful misunderstandings and to value people on their own terms?

6. Are there specific actions that your church will need to take to be effective in reaching out across cultures?

7. What proportion of your church's members is committed to cross-cultural outreach? How do you think that more members can catch the vision and get on board?

8. We have mostly thought about steps that majority culture members can take to bridge the divide. Can your church expect people from minority backgrounds to take steps too and, if so, what might those be?

9. What can a church do to make sure that non-English speaking background visitors to the church feel welcome?

10. How can and should leaders respond to obstructive attitudes, including racial prejudice, expressed by church members?

Notes

_____

_____

_____

_____

_____

_____

_____

_____

_____

_____

_____

_____

_____

_____

_____

_____

THE HOW

Module 4

CHANGING DRIVER SKILLS: INCREASING YOUR CULTURAL INTELLIGENCE AND SKILLS

4.1 Prayer | 4.2 Introduction | 4.3 Biblical reflection
4.4 Get educated! | 4.5 Pick up some skills
4.6 Summary | 4.7 Questions

4.1 Prayer

4.2 Introduction

In different cultures drivers may use the same signals to mean different things. In some cultures the use of a car's indicator does not mean, "I am about to change lanes," but "You can now overtake me." When churches are 'changing lanes' cross-culturally they need to make sure that decisions and the communication of what they are doing makes sense to those involved

— not merely to majority culture church members, but also to those from minority cultures. Cultural intelligence can be seen as the capability to adapt to a different culture. You probably already have some of this intelligence without realising it! Getting educated and developing some cultural skills will help you recognise what this is and how you can be even more effective in relating to people from other cultures.

4.3 Biblical reflection

Read Acts 17:16-34

1.   What indications are there that Paul had made the effort to understand the thought-world of Athenians?

2.   What motivated Paul not only to engage Athenians in debate but to do so in a way that connected with their cultural behaviour and understanding?

3.   In what ways do Paul's behaviour and words help us to understand how we should behave and speak when ministering to people across cultures?

4.4 Get educated!

For all of us, our own culture is usually invisible. We're very aware of the odd ways in which people from other backgrounds behave, but are rarely alert to our own presuppositions and behaviour, especially when we are the dominant ethnic group. However, spending some time reflecting on our own culture is always valuable as we interact with people from other cultural backgrounds.

Many Christians have found it very helpful to explore what culture is and how it works. With this kind of understanding, we'll be much better able to comprehend what's happening when cultures mix: why barriers appear and how we can get around or remove them. For example, you may wonder why some of your Asian friends are often late when invited. It may be because, in many cultures, punctuality is not nearly as important as stopping to talk to a friend who has phoned just as you're leaving to come to an appointment. By arming us with this kind of understanding, God can address the prejudices we may be carrying around and lead us to different ways of thinking and acting. As God convicts us, he can transfer those newly learned convictions in the cultural realm into behaviour that pleases him.

Don't imagine that this kind of transformation will happen quickly, for you or for the other members of your church or group. But do believe that it can happen, as many Christians have found and continue to find as God works in them to change attitudes and behaviour.

Like an iceburg, most of culture is "under the surface". Behaviour is visible, but underlying values, beliefs, worldviews and formative socialisation processes are not.

Culture has been described in many ways. One characteristic of culture is the way in which the shared values, beliefs and similar upbringings of a group of people influence 'the way we do things around here'. When we deal with people from other cultures, what usually strikes us is their behaviour. But behaviour is usually just the tip of the iceberg. Influencing behaviour are values that in turn have been largely shaped by beliefs and an upbringing that may be very different from your own. But there will almost always be a good reason for cultural behaviour we encounter and it won't be that people are behaving like that just to annoy us. In the case of your friends who routinely arrive late, the reason may be that for them people are more important than punctuality.

Patty Lane (2002, p. 47), in her helpful book *A Beginner's Guide to Crossing Cultures*, identifies and unpacks what she calls six cultural lenses. She says that "each culture has a unique way of seeing life and relationships. When we understand our own cultural lenses and the lenses of others, we are more likely to make friends with persons of other cultures". These are lenses

93

through which we all look at the same situation or people, but because of our culture, how we see people, things, and situations differs.

The 6 cultural lenses

A. Context

This lens includes environment, process, body language and appearance. Cultures range from high context to low context. Low context cultures, such as majority Australian culture, place relatively less importance on communication and messages of a non-verbal nature, and more importance on verbal communication. High context cultures, such as Korean culture, place a comparatively high degree of meaning on the setting: e.g. how a meeting is conducted, the quality of the venue, and how the presenter is dressed, etc.

B. Activity

Cultures are usually divided here into 'being' and 'doing' cultures. 'Being cultures' value relationships and quality of life, whilst 'doing cultures' value results and materialism (Lane 2002, p. 61). People in a 'doing culture' like Australia are interested in how many people attended a meeting and how many outcomes were achieved. People in a 'being culture' like Thailand's might be far more concerned about how people related to one another and whether they got to know one or two families better as a result of that meeting.

A Malaysian uni student in Western Australia always got the impression that the first priority of his Aussie pastor was evangelism, and friendship came second. In a NSW rural church that he and his wife attended later, where they were the only Asians, the pastor never had them in his home, although some congregation members did.

C. Authority

This lens divides cultures into authoritarian/formal and egalitarian/informal. In the former, unequal treatment of people is not only accepted but is expected and viewed as appropriate (Lane 2002, p. 73). Such cultures (e.g. Indian and Korean cultures) tend to have many rules for much of life and are characterised by respect for those in authority. Egalitarian cultures such as those of Australia, New Zealand and the Netherlands, for example, believe that all people have equal value and rights, though this is not always seen in practice. Such cultures often have low respect for people in authority, or expect people to earn respect, rather than merely receive it because of their position.

> Among people from the Indian subcontinent, one of the most serious 'sins' a cross-cultural worker can commit is to express anger openly. Alan Roland (2003, p. 279) observed how his patients in India kept "all kinds of angry feelings self-contained within the social etiquette of Indian hierarchical relationships." In sessions with patients he would see them raging "about a superior acting inappropriately toward them" and yet also see them "at work being completely deferential and cooperative with the same superior." This kind of behaviour is also common in Japanese and other Asian cultures.

D. Relationship

This lens usually categorises cultures as collectivistic or individualistic. People in collectivistic cultures see themselves as part of a group such as their family, tribe or community, and this greater whole is seen as important. Examples include Indian, Korean and some South American cultures. Individualistic cultures tend to see each person as an individual, and people relate to others on a one-to-one basis (Lane 2002, p. 86-87). To do a job by oneself, in one's own way, is usually valued in such cultures, which include Australian, North American, British and Scandinavian cultures.

 Our individuality lies in what we do not say." (as cited in Roland 2003, p. 280).

AKIHISA KONDO
JAPANESE PSYCHOANALYST

95

A refugee from Sudan is resettling in Melbourne. You ask him whether there are things about life in Australia he has found difficult. He would probably reply, "I am shocked by how rude people are when they travel on public transport. They don't talk to one other. They just sit and listen to music and read books."

E. Temporal

We're sure you've already faced this one many times if you have any cross-cultural experience, and it has been alluded to above. This lens sees time as either abundant or limited. The abundant view is that clock-watching is unhelpful and that we should be focused on more important aspects of life (Lane, p 99). This is the predominant view among Pacific Islanders or African people, for example. The limited viewpoint, seen amongst Australians and Western European cultures, is that time is a resource to be used wisely.

F. Worldview

Someone has said that if culture is a game of chess, worldview is the rules by which it runs. In *The Universe Next Door*, James Sire (2009, p. 4) identified a number of worldviews that form a set of first principles or presuppositions that people hold about reality. Each addresses in differing ways such fundamental questions as: Is there a God? What is the universe? Who am I? Where am I going? What are right and wrong? Does life have a purpose? Sire's worldviews include:

- Christian Theism, Deism (*people are but cogs in the Watchmaker's universe*)

- Naturalism (*people are only matter and machine*)

- Nihilism (*there is no meaning in life*)

- Existentialism (*people must create value and meaning in an absurd universe*)

- Eastern Pantheistic Monism *(people are one with the cosmos)*

- New Age *(people seeking a higher consciousness)*

- Postmodernism *(people create reality through language)*

The discussion of worldview has been the subject of numerous books. However, a very broad way of discriminating between worldviews is made possible if we divide cultures into those that are pre-modern, modern or postmodern. The category is not necessarily determined by religion. People from pre-modern cultures, like some Burmese minority or African cultures, are deeply influenced by tradition, mystery and experience and are more holistic in their view of life. Modern cultures tend to value the objective, the scientific, and are linear in their thinking. Postmodern people tend to determine truth subjectively, and want verification through experience. Both pre- and postmodern people accept the spiritual dimension more readily than do modernists. One example of how a pre-modern culture differs from a modern one is in explaining how disease is caused. A pre-modern culture might see the involvement of spirits, or previous bad deeds, while a modern person is sure that disease is caused by germs and poor care of one's body (Lane, pp 110-111).

As we look at culture through each of the six lenses described above, we find ourselves interacting with different value and belief systems. Understanding what other people value can have profound implications for the ways we choose to minister across cultures.

For many Chinese and Korean parents, having been profoundly shaped by Confucianism, it is important for their children to 'succeed'. Parents will invest considerable resources and push their children hard to succeed academically and secure what they feel are high-status professional positions. If a church finds itself with opportunities to minister to people of Chinese and Korean ethnicity, it may consider developing outreach ministries that help to meet such educational aspirations. So, for example, a church might provide after-school tutoring if it has members who have the requisite competence, in addition to *(cont.)*

---

being godly witnesses. At some point, however, especially as converted Chinese are being discipled, they, like all followers of Christ, will need to come to grips with the values of the kingdom of God. For Chinese, Japanese or Korean disciples this may, and often will, require some adjustment in the place accorded to success, education and wealth in one's own personal and family life.

Lingenfelter and Mayers (2003), and Hofstede (2001 and 2010), who pioneered the research of culture in the workplace, have helpfully identified and described some fundamental differences in cultural values. Appendix F: Reading List contains information on their work.

The above approaches to understanding culture are just a few of many helpful perspectives developed by cultural anthropologists and missiologists. The authors hope this introductory understanding of culture is already helping you to understand some of the strange or baffling cross-cultural interactions you've experienced. Our hope is that God may use this understanding to help you really see and follow what is going on, so that you can relate appropriately and in a deeply godly way across cultures.

4.5 Pick up some skills

Some of the skills you'll need are fairly obvious and will apply to other areas of your life, too. Skills that Anglo Aussie Christians sometimes overlook, because they see themselves as the dominant and even 'superior' culture, with much to contribute, include observing, listening and lifelong learning.

A. Observe

Firstly, take time to observe carefully how ethnic groups in your community and church relate to one another and to you. You might be surprised to find how different it is from the way Aussies tend to relate. One of the authors has found it a real eye-opener to attend an own language service led by one of the ethnic groups in his church. One-to-one, so many of this group are reserved and struggle with English as they interact with an Anglo Aussie, but in their own service and their own language, the devotion and leadership ability are plain to see.

B. Listen

Secondly, how good are we at listening? Do we monopolise or dominate conversations, and assume that we have plenty to give and to teach others and little to hear about? And do we fail to read the unspoken messages that many cultures give? We can learn such things, but it takes time, exposure, humility and patience.

C. Learn

Thirdly, we need to be learning continuously. We don't have all the answers, or the only, or best, approaches to worship, prayer, Bible study or hospitality. This book's authors have learnt, and continue to learn, so much from the 'strangers' with whom God has brought them into contact, including lessons about patience, respect for the elderly, perseverance, strong families and much more.

It would be unreasonable to think we can become proficient in many of the languages of the people in our circle of contacts and friends. But many Christians have found it very helpful to try to learn some key phrases. This can send a strong message that you value your friend's culture and language and are willing to be vulnerable as you botch up the pronunciation and to become a learner. Asking your friends to write some phrases out for you is a good way to strengthen relationships and to learn about one another. In addition, common phrases in many languages are usually available on the internet.

Learning about our friends' beliefs is also important. We may not learn about all the major religions in depth, but once you know the kinds of people you'll be working among most, you might focus in on the abundant relevant information on the net, and in books. John Dickson's (2014)

A Spectator's Guide to World Religions is especially helpful. Once again, as you get to know ethnic minority contacts more closely, they'll be very happy to explain what they believe and why. Unlike many Anglo Aussies, religion is definitely not a no-go area for many from other faith backgrounds.

> An Anglo Aussie Christian woman regularly visited a lady from the Middle East who lived nearby. After a few months, the friendship really deepened and one day the lady placed her hand on our friend's knee as they sat on the couch discussing something. This was a little off-putting for the Aussie friend, but was probably a sign of how comfortable the neighbour was with her.

D. Practise hospitality

Lastly, hospitality is perhaps a forgotten or little-used skill among many city-dwelling Anglo Aussies. Our society is often so individualistic and both spouses are often working long hours outside the home, so that people can be too weary or preoccupied to show hospitality. You're maybe already aware how hospitable your minority ethnic friends are, even though they may have very basic means to live on. Hence, for us to show hospitality is an important part of developing and deepening relationships and showing the love of God. "But what will I feed them?" you may be wondering. You could ask your friends about food preferences, which will lead to other great topics, or you could decide to arrange an afternoon tea, or go out for a meal, till you get to know one another better. If you make cultural mistakes, they will often be forgiven, but remember to learn from them. When your friends begin to tell you about a *faux pas* you've made, it could well be a good sign — they like and trust you enough to tell you.

> A migrant from South-East Asia pointed out how different hospitality is in his country. He felt that people were more hospitable there and said that in his culture, one could drop in on a friend without a prior arrangement. Timing of visits was much more flexible, also. (cont.)

Hossein Adibi (1998, p. 128) observes: "To Iranians, Australians are inhospitable. (They)have been invited to Iranian parties and official functions but they never invite Iranians in return."

Hospitality

4.6 Summary

Increasing our cultural intelligence helps focus our attitude, thinking and skill development in ways that encourage us to behave sensitively and appropriately towards people of different backgrounds. It will also help us to acquire and practise relevant cross-cultural skills. If a church is to be effective in ministry across cultures its leaders too will play a crucial role in addressing improper attitudes and behaviour, both in themselves and in their congregation members, and identifying ways to equip themselves and their church members with necessary knowledge and skills. It is this area of leadership that is discussed in the next module.

4.7 Questions

1. Identify 3–5 cultural differences you have observed or experienced. For each difference:

   a. What values might be expressed through the different cultural behaviour you've encountered? (You could look again at the value ranges identified by Lingenfelter and Mayers, and Hofstede).

   b. What opportunities are there for you and/or your church to engage in ministry across cultures?

   c. What knowledge and skills do you need to develop to be effective in such ministry?

   d. What steps do you or your church need to take to be equipped with the knowledge and skills needed?

2. You plan to hold a lunch for a multi-ethnic group. How might the makeup of the group affect how you go about this?

3. Try filling in the table below and then discuss your answers as a group.

Cultural lens	Points of tension between different cultures
Context	
Being/Doing	

Cultural lens	Points of tension between different cultures
Authority	
Relationships	
Time	
Worldview	

Notes

Module 5

CHANGING ROAD MANAGEMENT: THE IMPORTANCE OF LEADERSHIP & MANAGEMENT FOR MINISTRY ACROSS CULTURES

5.1 Prayer

5.2 Introduction

Good drivers expect that the people who construct the roads and set out the rules for driving on them have given road safety and efficiency considerable thought. Similarly, it is important for church leaders to consider their congregations' profiles carefully, to acquire cross-cultural understanding and to lead in ways that are most appropriate. And it's also vital that members support and follow their leaders as they direct the ministry. The importance of leadership was alluded to at the end of the previous module. This current module examines leadership, explores the influence of culture on leadership and how leaders can be more effective in their pursuit of a ministry across cultures. The module highlights how leadership actions and outcomes can be misinterpreted by people from other cultures and how leaders, in carrying out their tasks, duties and responsibilities, can act with cultural sensitivity, minimise misunderstandings and promote mutual understanding, act in a culturally inclusive manner and positively promote ministry across cultures in the congregation.

5.3 Biblical reflection

Read Galatians 2

1.   Who were some of the foremost leaders in the early church and what were the leadership roles of Peter and Paul? (verses 7-10)

2.   What went wrong with Peter's leadership and why? (verses 11-14)

3.   What does this passage teach about the kind of leadership needed when ministering across cultures?

5.4 Leadership and leaders

Leadership implies that there are at least two parties in a relationship. One party leads, the other is led. Either party may be made up of one or more persons. In a church, leadership is not merely exercised by ordained persons. In addition to the minister or pastor there may be leaders such as elders, deacons, the music coordinator, small group leaders and the Sunday school coordinator. At a less obvious level, leadership is also exercised by welcomers, visitation carers, the morning tea coordinator, the property maintenance coordinator and others.

Who is a leader? It is someone who leads others, whether formally or informally. A leader also bears responsibility for others, whether it is for their wellbeing or the work that they do. For example, the welcoming team co-ordinator is in a formal leadership role, while the welcomers are informal leaders. The coordinator leads the welcomers and bears responsibility for the way in which welcoming is done. The welcomer makes a difference to the wellbeing of people who come through the doors of the church. Informal leadership is often overlooked, yet it is critical to achieving key goals. It is integral to any discussion of church leadership. An analogy is to think of formal leaders as the bricks of a church building and informal leaders as the cement that holds the bricks together. Both types of materials are equally important components of the church. Both are leaders.

> A church has been engaging for some years in various programs reaching out to various ethnic groups in the community. A lay person was formally tasked with bringing together these programs so as to encourage the wider church to own this ministry, as well as to assist individual team leaders in feeling that their programs are a vital part of the wider church. Informally, another lay person was co-opted to assist with the formally appointed leader. Through the combined responsibilities and commitment of the formal and informal leaders, the objective of a church-wide ownership of the ethnic outreach programs was achieved in the space of one year. Both the formal leader (brick) and informal leader (cement) are integral to this achievement.

Responsibility involves a sense of purpose. To accept one's responsibilities as a leader is to commit oneself to achieving certain ends or goals. To do this, a leader may insist on or appeal to his or her authority. Alternatively, the leader may depend on persuasion and other gentler approaches. Leaders will usually combine these different approaches in some way. The purpose of leadership then is for the leader to exercise authority and/or skills to encourage the desired behaviour of the other. The aim is to motivate the other to behave in ways that contribute to the achievement of certain goals, which includes the goal of promoting the wellbeing of the other.

Have confidence in your leaders and submit to their authority, because they keep watch over you as those who must give an

account. Do this so that their work will be a joy, not a burden, for that
would be of no benefit to you.

HEBREWS 13:17

As the above text reminds us, God will require those in positions of pastoral
authority to give an account of how responsibly they have watched over
the flock entrusted to them. This includes equipping God's people through
the ministry of God's Word, protecting them from false teaching, administering church discipline when needed, encouraging the saints to live godly
lives and building a community characterised by Spirit-produced love and
unity that glorifies God before a watching and lost world. Given our focus
in this book, our present concern is with an exercise of leadership that ena-
bles churches and their congregation members to be God-honouring and
fruitful as they minister to people across cultures.

5.5 Cultural understandings of leadership

As we saw in our last module, the way in which people live their lives will
be an expression of the way they view the world, depending on the cultural
lenses they are using. Underlying values and beliefs vary from culture to
culture. It is inevitable that people's cultures shape their understanding of
what constitutes a good leader.

> Steve, an Australian with high-level theological degrees, was invited to
> join the faculty of a small Bible college in Pakistan. He would present
> them with a Bible passage and invite them to debate different ways of
> interpreting and understanding the text. He was disappointed with the
> response. They kept saying to him, "You tell us what it says." The stu-
> dents were not impressed with Steve. From their perspective it seemed
> that Steve was not a good leader because he lacked authority.

The point being made in the above story should be kept in mind: effective
leaders consider the culture of the listeners and attempt to modify their
behaviours accordingly, especially when churches reach out to first generation migrants.

5.6 Planning for a multi-ethnic church

The church leadership has a planning role. Godly leaders articulate what the church as a collective group of Bible-believers should and can do and the goals it strives to achieve. For example, at a broad level leaders might remind believers that "the chief end of (people) is to glorify God and to enjoy him forever" (Shorter Catechism, Westminster Confession). This statement sets before God's people a vision of what their lives are meant to be. Godly leaders will take deliberate action to enable God's people to live lives that glorify God and enable them to delight in him. In church services they will deliberately incorporate well-chosen and appropriate hymns, prayers, Bible readings and a sermon. In church life they will establish Bible study and fellowship groups and other structures such as pastoral care and one-to-one discipling relationships. But this in turn involves using a vast array of resources — time-commitments from people, song lyrics, musical instruments, people with musical skills, Bibles, places to meet and so on. In short, all competent leaders set before their people a vision, employ deliberate means in realising that vision and draw upon or acquire the necessary resources needed for the employment of those means.

The authors recognise that some churches are uncomfortable with developing formalised strategic plans. For some churches, such plans are not a common tool. Or perhaps this smacks of treating the church like a business operation. In no way are we encouraging church leaders to lead a church in the same way that managers run a business. But we need to recognise that, because ministry across cultures involves swimming against the current, it requires a high degree of intentionality.

> A church with a large potential for interethnic ministries did not find it necessary to have multi-ethnicity as a core value of the church, believing that minority ethnic groups in the community who chose to attend this church would naturally weave into the status quo of the mainly Anglo-centric church. The leaders felt confident that the congregation members would welcome, care for and embrace everyone equally, regardless of ethnicity, as one in the Christian family, and they *(cont.)*

trusted that ethnic minority members as Christians would easily fit
into what was, after all, the same church family in Christ. Years went by
and the church remained mystified that ethnic minorities were coming
and going from the church and not a single minority-background lay
leader had emerged to participate more fully in the life of the church.
An intentional focus on this problem, leading to an explicit statement of
multi-ethnicity as a core value of the church, was the turning point for it
to become more relevant to its community.

For this reason it is desirable for leaders to develop a more formalised
strategic plan to ensure that ministry across cultures is not neglected or
minimised among the other demands of ministry and church life. Such a
strategic plan should consist of the following:

1. A vision (reflecting the church's values and mindful of the
    environment in which the church finds itself).

2. A plan to realise the vision (activities, structures and processes that
    support the vision).

3. The resources to implement the plan (paid or volunteer human
    resources, finance, technology, property, etc.).

God-honouring churches are shaped by God's Word and must avoid ungodly conformity to the world. Christians are called to be holy as God is
holy, which entails being different, being salt and light in a dark world. This
means such churches will not make a cult out of relevance. As Os Guinness
(2003, p. 15) observes in *Prophetic Untimeliness*: "By our uncritical pursuit
of relevance we have actually courted irrelevance." But this does not justify
ignorance of our environment. We have only to think of Jesus' confronta-
tions with the religious leaders of his day and of Paul in Athens to see how
churches must familiarise themselves with their environment if they are to
be effective in ministry to people, including ministry across cultures.

Leadership planning needs to keep in mind not only the external environment of the church but also its internal environment. The latter involves a
consideration of the church's resources, structure and culture.

Figure 2: Imaginary Church SWOT Analysis

	Helpful	Unhelpful
Internal	• Good building facilities • Excellent location of buildings • Some key members are returned missionaries • Congregation open to cross-cultural involvement • Strong youth group etc.	• No past cross-cultural experience as a church • Some church members are negatively disposed towards this ministry • Welcoming and hospitality ministries need considerable development • Poor car-parking facilities etc.
External	• Many migrants want to learn English • Possibility of incorporating a non-English speaking background church into our church community • Many migrants receptive to door-knocking etc.	• Lack positive relationships with community leaders • Few people from ethnic minority backgrounds living in the church's vicinity • Mormons and Jehovah's Witnesses are very active in this area etc.

In seeking to set their church's situation against the external environment affecting the church, many churches have found it helpful to conduct a SWOT analysis (see Fig 2 above), that is, identifying, listing and assessing Strengths (internal advantages that give the church an edge), Weaknesses (internal disadvantages that hamper the church), Opportunities (external advantages that can be capitalised on in developing God-honouring ministry), and Threats (external disadvantages that hamper fruitful ministry).

In planning the church's strategy, the composition of the planning team would benefit from reflecting the cultural mix in the church's environment (see also Section 6.6). There are often cultural experts who are very knowledgeable about people from other cultures. Such people have much to offer the planning team. Cultural experts, however, will be the first to admit that it is impossible to understand all cultures, or to be completely 'the other' in matters of culture. Inviting people from the other cultures in the community to form a culturally diverse team will enable the planning to better capture the diversity that is required to serve and create the diverse church. For example, in designing a pastoral support program for people in grief, churches will agree that people should not suffer alone. Yet cultures differ in the degree to which 'alone' means 'alone'. It is only as a church involves people from particular cultures that it can gain insights into subtle cultural differences that can be incorporated into the grief care program. Cultural experts can be sourced from church members in the congregation, members of other churches in the local community, or cultural informants from the culture that the church is planning to reach.

> An Australian-Korean woman suddenly and unexpectedly lost her husband. She had been an integral part of a multi-ethnic church for a number of years and had contributed to the growth of multi-ethnic ministry in this church. There was no lack of kindness and love shown to this much-appreciated lady by the Anglo Aussie members of this church. However, the lady observed one distinct cultural difference. In contrast to the Korean members of the congregation, when Anglo Aussie women visited her to express support they did not stay the night. It was the staying overnight by Korean church members that made her feel fully supported.

Planning for a multi-ethnic church without involving people from minority cultures has unfortunate consequences. It reinforces the view that the majority culture knows best about how to include others in their church. Excluding minority members from the planning process communicates an air of superiority, a belief that is further reinforced when there are memories of a colonial history. The mono-cultural planning team also conveys the patronising message that something is being done for the other. This engenders a divisive feeling, the sense that the church is the home of the majority culture, but an adopted home of everyone else.

In a particular Anglican church, research during the planning process showed that first generation ethnic Chinese were a growing presence in the community. All the church staff members were Anglo Aussies, and they recognised their limitations in effectively reaching out to this ethnic group. A Chinese parish councillor was appointed (rather than elected) onto the parish council by the senior minister and she provided input on the needs of the Chinese community. In subsequent years, she continued in the role, but as an elected member in her own right, and contributed information and ideas on how best to have a more culturally inclusive church.

5.7 Organising a culturally inclusive church

Church leaders also have an organising role. Organising realises the plan of the church and involves structuring church resources, activities and workflow. This includes being clear about the activities and processes that will help the church to see the realisation of its goal of ministry across cultures, identifying required tasks, sequencing those tasks, identifying suitable people to carry them out, assigning tasks to individuals, clustering tasks and developing structures that will enable the church to carry out this ministry both competently and fruitfully.

Informal social-networking technology such as WhatsApp can also play a role in developing helpful structures that will reinforce relationships, enable responsiveness to pastoral needs and strengthen networking among church members. Other technologies such as Facebook, Skype and Facetime have varying uses and can be considered.

Four first generation migrant women who have found their place in an evolving multi-ethnic church identified a need to minister specifically to divorced women. A WhatsApp leadership group among these women was established to manage the organisation and ministry of this group of women. The technology allowed the leaders to get quickly organised amidst their multiple commitments to family and work and to stay close to one another for mutual encouragement and sharing, as they *(cont.)*

support a highly demanding ministry.

In a church plant in Sydney's west, the introduction of a WhatsApp group among the Friday afternoon sports for the youth in the community has allowed the leaders to be connected with members more than just once a week.

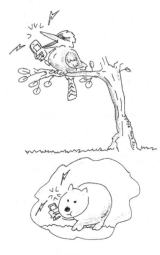

Mobile Apps

In churches that are committed to a plan for reaching out across cultures, leaders face a particular organisational challenge. It is possible that distinct groups and activities may simply 'do their own thing' and be out of step with where the church is headed. Leaders must strive to ensure that all groups and activities are in alignment with the church's vision and plan. For the sake of the church's mission, some church members may even need to be encouraged to think and pray about joining a different group either instead of or in addition to whatever current group commitments they have, in order to produce a more inclusive and diverse church community..

An Anglo Aussie woman and a migrant volunteer initiated an outreach program to migrant women in the community close to a suburban church. The aim was to offer friendship to migrant women and connect them with each other for mutual support. Within a year, ESL classes commenced in the church. A Simple English Bible Study group that ran parallel with the Sunday morning family service time was subsequently started. Through the years these and various cross-cultural ministries operated as stand-alone activities. They had a bumpy ride. Despite the commitment of various leaders, attendances some years were better than in other years. Leaders of this outreach ministry were feeling unappreciated and approaching burn-out. Ten years later an International Ministry team was formed that worked on connecting these various ministry activities into a cohesive and supportive body. New activities, such as a prayer group and a drop-in morning tea group, were introduced. Ministry leaders were encouraged to attend each other's activities so that visitors became familiar with them and would feel more welcome to join in their activities. Where possible, multi-ethnic teams at all levels were formed, giving migrants the choice of making friends not only with their own people but also with people from the mainstream culture. This also had the effect of narrowing the gaps between these various ministries and the wider church. Numbers in each activity took a leap. There was stability and growth from year to year. New friendships were formed among the leaders.

As leaders reflect on the way their church is organised, they need to consider the cultural and ethnic composition of the groups that make up the church. There are real benefits in ensuring that the cultural composition of these groups adequately reflects the range of intended cultures and ethnicities to which the church wishes to minister. For instance, visual impressions make a strong impact. If the ethnic composition of the worship group is reflective of those the church is aiming to reach, then the message is loud and clear that the church is indeed serious in its commitment to this. A worship group that looks primarily to be of one culture misses the opportunity to use this simple strategy to communicate a very important value of the church: that of welcoming, involving and valuing people of all cultures.

Left to themselves, friendships and fellowships across cultures do not just happen. 'Birds of a feather flock together' is an apt saying in this instance.

While organisers need to consider intentionally the optimal mix of cultures in any group activities and to strive intentionally to achieve this mix, church members can intentionally move into groups that appear to be predominantly of one culture which is different from their own. While many individuals may feel they lack the courage to do this, it is often easier for a member of the majority group to break into a mono-cultural minority group than it is for a minority group member to break into a mono-cultural majority group. Try it: you may be pleasantly surprised by the reception you receive!

In a predominantly Anglo Aussie church, four members of an eight-person team of international lay leaders were Anglo Aussie and the remaining members were of Asian descent. The Anglo Aussie members intentionally sought out groups of Asians at morning tea time after the service to introduce and/or socialise with them. In due course, the Asians began to naturally gravitate towards groups where at least one of the Anglo Aussies was present, regardless of the composition of the groups. Cross-cultural friendships and fellowships began to evolve naturally from there, but it took an intentional move to get it started. One such cross-cultural fellowship group continues to meet annually years after members had left to pursue ministry opportunities elsewhere.

5.8 Inclusive leadership style

Leadership is about connectedness, between the vision and the leader, and between the leader and the people being led. Effective leaders have their finger on the pulse. They know what is happening in the lives of the members of their congregation. To do so, they are connected and they stay connected. They are involved and are able to spread their connection by meeting with people at all levels. Where necessary, they connect people with one another and refer others to external services. Referrals are not the end of the relationship; the relationship of caring and concern is ongoing, even if the responsibility to help is extended to others in a better position to do so. Leaders and those to whom people might be referred become partners in the caring relationship.

A pastor referred one of his church members for counselling. The church member embarked on a course of counselling over several months. In that period, the pastor did not enquire into the content of the counselling but kept in touch with the church member, showing care and concern that the counselling was working for her. She not only felt cared for by this pastor who referred her to an external resource for help, she also continued to feel cared for by the church when, from time to time, the pastor enquired about how she was progressing.

If church members are to have confidence in their leaders and in the strategic actions taken by their leaders, then it is imperative that leaders involve themselves in the lives of their church members, both formally and informally. On the one hand, a wider source of information is captured that contributes to more effective and relevant decisions being made and on the other hand it allows for the ownership and full engagement of everyone with the goals of the church.

The core of connectedness is involvement. But the boundaries of involvement are different for different cultures. Asian-Australian leaders, for example, are often especially available and willing to be involved in the wider family and other affairs of the people they minister to. The ministry and personal relationship boundary is practically nonexistent. Accordingly, from an Anglo Aussie perspective, more is demanded of Asian-Australian leaders in general and they seem to be more involved in the lives of others. By contrast, from an Asian standpoint, Anglo Aussie leaders appear to be more distant and less interested. Such cultural differences, when unnoticed and unacknowledged, undermine the efforts of churches trying to build a cohesive multi-ethnic church community.

An Anglo Aussie Bible study leader was much admired for her ability to engage with individuals at a personal level. What's more, she was clearly gifted as a Bible teacher. These gifts were consistently evident in Bible Study meetings. Outside of regular Bible Study times, however, this leader was not available. Emails were generally unanswered *(cont.)*

and invitations to coffee were usually declined or ignored. Contrast this with another Bible Study leader, an Asian. She was appreciated for her Bible teaching but more so for her pastoral care initiatives. She met with each member of the group one-on-one at least once a term, and at other times in twos or threes. To the Australian members, the behaviour of the Anglo Aussie leader was much more acceptable than to the Asian members. Regarding the Asian leader, Asian members perceived her as doing her job well; to some of the Aussies, she was almost being 'cultish'. The Anglo Aussie leader was guided by her individualistic background that more clearly delineated her responsibilities from her private life; for the Asian leader with a collectivistic background, this boundary was far less clear-cut.

Asians often expect to be told the limits of their responsibilities and hence what to do rather than just be given guidelines when seeking leaders' inputs. Leaders need to be aware of the different expectations of their varied congregation members from different cultures, including in situations of giving pastoral care.

Lifeline has a strong philosophy of not telling callers what to do but providing them with guidelines to support them emotionally through empathic listening and other skills. This is supposed to clarify their thinking, so that options can be explored and informed decisions can be made. Lifeline's equivalent in Malaysia is the Befrienders, whose tagline is 'care and advice'. Many people from an Asian background feel that a counselling service that does not include the giving of sound advice is not a caring service.

Across cultures there may be conflict as to what constitutes appropriate care. For example, South Sudanese families will often be very private and unwilling to be open about family issues with non-family members. Many South Sudanese have a high respect for elders in their community and it is such elders who would be asked to deal with conflicts in families and in the community rather than perhaps an Anglo Aussie care worker. But the migration experience makes it more difficult for South Sudanese living in

Australia to function as they would if living in South Sudan. For many older South Sudanese, the experience of displacement has damaged their ability to carry out their traditional roles among the South Sudanese community in Australia. This means that it is additionally difficult for the younger South Sudanese living in Australia to deal with conflicts in their homes and community. Leadership style needs to be adapted so as to elicit the most desirable responses from those who come from a variety of cultural backgrounds.

At the risk of over-generalising, it can be said that Anglo Aussie leaders are more consultative and Asian-Australian leaders more directive. It is not uncommon for newly arrived Asians to view such an Anglo Aussie leader as weak and for Anglo Aussies new to Asian culture to view the Asian-Australian leader negatively as over-controlling. Asian-Australian workers not used to the Anglo Aussie leadership style and expecting more direction can be viewed by Anglo Aussies as lacking in initiative and confidence. Anglo Aussie workers not used to the Asian leadership style and expecting their input to carry more weight can be perceived by Asian-Australians as being disrespectful and overly-confident. To get the most out of Anglo Aussie workers, invite them whenever possible to contribute their thoughts to issues and problems when they first arise. Anglo Aussies, like Asian-Australians, expect the leader to bear ultimate responsibility for making decisions, but they like more input into the process. Asian-Australians also like to provide input but this is often done in informal settings, with decisions formalised in meetings. It is therefore not uncommon for Anglo Australian social situations to mainly be about socialising, with 'talking shop' being frowned upon. For the Asian-Australian this boundary is blurred: work and social talk are intertwined.

Churches committed to ministry across cultures are busy with events and activities that are very social, and these make up the 'glue' of the church. Informal events are important and are often overlooked, and yet without them, the 'bricks' are in great danger of not supporting and sustaining the structure for growth. Strong community spirit and *(cont.)*

ties are seen in churches with more informal social events than formal activities. 'Keep the ears to the ground' by keeping in touch with the whole cross section of people formally and informally. Organise face time to meet with each group throughout the year. Such events as afternoon teas for newcomers, and short courses led by the leaders, provide important opportunities for leaders to meet in small groups with newcomers and allow everyone the opportunity to be known and to know others.

Another key task of the leader is to mobilise the work of others to accomplish goals. Every cultural group needs teams of people to accomplish their overall goal. Team work helps us to achieve more than the sum of the parts, and hence makes it possible for us to achieve more with less. When working cross-culturally, team work is acted out differently depending on the culture of the team members. Give a group of Anglo Aussies a project, and they will quickly divide up the different tasks that need to be performed and then bring the completed parts of the project together to produce the outcome. Give the same project to a group of Asian-Australians, and they will also divide up the different tasks but will then be intricately involved with each other's task – contributing and checking each other's work as they go along. Hence, individual contribution and task ownership is clearer with the Anglo Aussie team than with the Asian-Australian team. However, members of the Asian-Australian team feel greater ownership for the project as a whole than Anglo Aussies do. There is a greater tendency for Asian-Australians to feel 'left to their own devices' when working in mixed teams, while Anglo Aussies may feel there is too much interference in how they do their job.

A migrant was appointed by the minister to participate in a strategic planning meeting. Except for this one migrant, the group was made up of white Anglo Aussie men and women. As a member of a collective culture operating in a predominantly individualistic environment, it was difficult for the new migrant member to feel a sense of *(cont.)*

belonging despite the efforts made by the other members to be inclusive. One individual took it upon herself to form a personal friendship with the migrant, visiting and inviting her to visit in her own home. In a few short weeks, these social visits provided lots of opportunities for the migrant to communicate her thoughts and visions for the church to this other member of the planning group. In due course, this friend became the mouthpiece of the migrant and many of the migrant member's ideas were communicated at the planning meetings and incorporated into the planning process.

5.9 Summary

Leadership is a universal phenomenon, but leadership style is situational. No single leadership style works well in all situations. What makes leadership effective varies from culture to culture. Leadership profiles vary from culture to culture, people's expectations of their leaders differ and people from different cultures admire different qualities in their leaders. There is scope for all of us, whether in a highly visible formal leadership position such as Bible Study leading or in a less visible informal leadership position such as cleaning up in the kitchen, to develop our own style of effective cross-cultural leadership.

We are all leaders in one way or another regardless of our cultural backgrounds. It is hoped that this module offers some practical approaches that everyone in the church, whatever their function — planning, organising or evaluating, and whatever their position or role — formal or informal — can take towards helping their church become more multi-ethnic and hence more relevant to the people in their community.

The following module offers further lessons the authors have learnt from the examples of some more fruitful churches they have come across in the course of their varied ministries.

5.10 Questions

1. What do you understand by the statement that everyone is a leader?

2. What are the main functions of a leader?

3. To which of the leader's functions identified in this module do the activities you are doing belong? How is the way you are carrying out your activity culturally inclusive? If there is anything you can do differently to make it even easier for people from other backgrounds to join in, how will you do that?

4. Can you identify who in your church is responsible for and/or is involved in each of the leader's functions identified above? Describe how each of the functions is being performed by the various individuals and give an example of how culture influences each of the functions. What can be done differently to make the church friendlier to a greater variety of people?

5. Are leaders made or born? Discuss.

6. How can you support the leaders at all levels of your church's ministries?

Notes

_____

_____

_____

_____

_____

_____

_____

_____

_____

_____

_____

_____

_____

_____

_____

_____

_____

_____

_____

THE HOW & WHEN

Module 6

CHANGING THE GPS: WHERE TO FROM HERE?

6.1 Prayer

6.2 Introduction

In Appendix C we ask for your self-evaluation in terms of where you think you and your church currently sit against the background of engaging with and embracing people from all cultures. Having worked your way through this book, either in a group or on your own, the authors ask that you now answer the next two questions:

QUESTIONS

1. In which lane are you (and your church) currently travelling?

2. In the next 12 months, where would you like to see yourself and your church stand in regards to this vital ministry of sharing the love of Jesus with all the various groups of people in your community?

If you decide that there is room for you to change lane, the authors offer tips and handy hints in this module to encourage you on your way. It should be noted that the tips below apply not only to churches that want to become more multi-ethnic, but also to all biblically-based congregations. However, where appropriate, the authors have commented particularly on the special issues encountered in multi-ethnic churches.

6.3 Biblical reflection

Read Acts 10:9-29

A. Coping with change: Peter

In a history-making vision Peter was required by God to undertake an enormous change.

1. What was this change?

   a. In the vision? (see especially verses 12-14)

   b. In reality? (see especially verse 28)

2. What was Peter's reaction to this prospect of change? (see verse 14)

3. Why did Peter find it so enormously difficult to deal with the change required of him?

    a. In the vision? (see especially Deuteronomy 14:3-21)

    b. In reality? (see especially verse 28)

4. What truths did Peter need to learn in order to cope with this change?

    a. Acts 10:28

    b. Acts 10:34

    c. Acts 10:47; 11:17

5. How did the early church change as a result of what God did? (see Acts 11:18-21)

B. Coping with Change: Us

1. What changes might God be requiring of his people here in Australia?

2. How does Peter's experience provide guidelines for us regarding ministry to people from other cultural and ethnic backgrounds?

6.4 Know the purpose of your existence

As Bible-believers, regardless of whether we consider ourselves leaders or not, we are given a clear understanding of what our end goal is. The Apostle Paul says in his first letter to the Corinthians, Chapter 10, verse 31:

"So whether you eat or drink or whatever you do, do it all for the glory of God."

The ultimate goal of all believers is to contribute to the glory of God, whatever our secondary goals and means of achieving this goal may be.

Immediately following the directive to glorify God, the apostle Paul goes on to caution us in verses 32 and 33:

"Do not cause anyone to stumble, whether Jews, Greeks or the church of God — even as I try to please everyone in every way. For I am not seeking my own good but the good of many, so that they may be saved."

Paul is saying that we are not to behave in ways that will cause anyone to walk away from God, whatever their backgrounds may be. Not only must we avoid erecting barriers against the people of any culture ('Jews' and 'Greeks'), but we must also avoid causing the 'church of God' to stumble. It follows from this that we have a responsibility to behave towards one another, and to lead and manage the church, in ways that do not cause stumbling. This responsibility raises two questions for all of us: how are we to behave so as not to cause individuals (whatever their backgrounds) to stumble, and how are we to manage the affairs of the church so that it does not stumble? What is good behaviour and what is good church management? The following tips are designed to help.

6.5 Prepare yourself and your church to go the next step

For everyone in the church, when you know that your ultimate goal in life is to glorify God, to make him known by building relationships to be of service to one another and to share his love for everyone, you can start to make preparations for accomplishing each of these worthy goals. Keep focusing on the intrapersonal factor of centring yourself on God. Whatever goal you are formulating, and whatever knowledge and skills you are acquiring to help you be more effective at ministering across cultures, lay them at Jesus' feet and submit them all to the will of God.

Work on your interpersonal capabilities of connecting with people in your church and community who are different from yourself — people with different personalities, cultural, ethnic and social backgrounds, history, intellectual and physical abilities, gender, sexual orientation, age, etc. Build a diverse community. We don't have to accept everyone's beliefs, but we can accept everyone as they are, imperfect and sinful as we are ourselves.

Some people in the church have the added responsibility of strategic planning for the church. Not all pastors and leaders will have this gift, but such planning needs to be undertaken if the church is to move forward as a group of people who pool their spiritual gifts and resources, in dependence on God, to glorify him in reaching out across cultures. Gifts, knowledge and skills are available, sometimes from within the church, sometimes from outside. It is a wise leader who knows where the gaps lie between his needs and his capabilities and who allocates resources accordingly.

After considerable research and consultation, the local church agreed to plant a new service in Sydney's west that would appeal to people of all cultures from the surrounding area. Over the course of nine months, the Chinese minister met with his core team each week to teach, pastor, encourage, train and equip the members for the task ahead. When the weekly services commenced, the core team had remained intact and the church plant is seeing non-Christians coming to the services.

In another church, a Chinese member planned to reach the residents on her street to invite them to attend various programs in the church. She planned to walk the street at least three times a week to meet her neighbours. As part of her planning, she contacted people who might pray and/or walk with her. She very successfully invited a constant stream of visitors to the church.

6.6 Set up a diverse team

This point has been discussed in Module 5 (Section 5.6) and is reiterated here to highlight its significance. Culture is a social construct and, unless one is born within a particular culture and immersed in it from childhood, critical nuances of meanings are invariably easy to overlook. To capture the variety of cultural views to be incorporated into the strategic planning process, it is vital that the planning team is diverse. With a diverse team in place, choices of activities for each of the key ministry areas, and the ways these are carried out, will then be much more relevant to the diversity in the community.

In implementing the plan, the face of the church is also something to be considered. The church that is committed to ministry across cultures can best walk the talk by having the value it places on this commitment reflected in all areas of its functions and at all levels. Visitors and other outsiders looking in from without are easily and strongly influenced by visual images, which impact on their perception of how serious and truly welcoming the church is towards those in the community from different ethnic and cultural backgrounds. If most of those in up-front leadership roles and heading up ministries are from a particular ethnic background, newcomers from other ethnic groups will not feel truly at home.

Team diversity may not always be possible, especially when the church first embarks on ministry across cultures. If this is the case, then consider co-opting culturally appropriate people from outside the church, whether for a fixed term or permanently. Many churches and their members are outward looking and are willing to release their own people to serve in needier churches, for the sake of the greater good of the wider church. Denominations may have regional strategies to facilitate this type of strategic approach to support their overall growth.

> The English speaking congregation of a Korean church set itself to attract non-Koreans. To that end it asked an Anglo Aussie lecturer from a Bible College, with considerable cross-cultural experience, to commit himself to leading their service each Sunday and helping them to become more culturally diverse. He was able to bring a number of students from the college with him to assist him in this venture. This immediately meant that the up-front look of the congregation was no longer only Korean. The church was able to become much more culturally diverse as a result of this initiative.

6.7 Expect different decision-making styles

A. Degree of consultation

Culture plays a role in decision-making. Culture influences whether decisions are made collaboratively by the group or autocratically by the leader.

Japanese people tend to consult widely and make corporate decisions; Anglo Aussies also like to consult widely but the decisions are usually in the hands of the leaders; and Australian leaders from the Indian subcontinent are likely to be decisive in their decisions with less input from the team than their Anglo Aussie counterparts.

B. Timeline for decisions

Culture also influences how quickly decisions are made. Anglo Aussies are usually quicker in making up their minds while Egyptian-Australian leaders tend to take more time in decision-making. Similarly, Asian-Australians spend a lot more time deliberating, but once the decision is made, its implementation is rapid. The significance of decisiveness is that with some cultures, rushing the decision-making process can be viewed as trivialising the relationships between the parties, failing to value the views of all, and not giving the issue at hand enough importance. Where decisions are more autocratic, less time tends to be required.

C. Nature of the process

Culture has implications for how, where and when decisions are made. Unlike the Anglo Aussie decision-making process, where much is discussed at meetings and decisions are made at subsequent meetings, many other cultures, much is discussed and agreed in informal gatherings, and meetings are merely where decisions are formalised. Leaders working in a multi-ethnic context need to be aware of this.

D. Objectivity vs. Subjectivity

Where cultures are more collectivistic than individualistic, decision-making can be more subjective rather than objective. Where subjective decision-making is predominant, feelings and intuition take priority over facts. This is not to say that rationality has no place to play in these cultures, but that emotions and instincts are more highly regarded and are factored more prominently into the process.

E. Tolerance for uncertainty

Cultures also differ in the degree to which they tolerate uncertainty. In some cultures, leaders often cope with high levels of uncertainty. Such leaders will often make decisions more readily and be prepared to accept greater risk. In cultures where leaders characteristically have a low tolerance for dealing with uncertainty, such as Japan and Pakistan, the tendency will be to stick to the tried and tested route. Anglo Aussies are often more innovative and decisive than some other groups; Asian-Australians tend to be more conservative and tentative in decision-making. Therefore, before asking your church members to make decisions, consider their cultural background. Giving some of them the liberty to decide may put them under tremendous stress rather than empower them. Putting before them what they see as risky options may create anxiety rather than give them a chance to shine.

F. Motivation

An apparent lack of motivation to make decisions should not be mistaken as a lack of interest. Some cultures have a stronger belief that outcomes are within their control (an internal locus of control), while others feel that outcomes are in the hands of forces outside of their control, such as fate (external locus of control). Anglo Aussies have a stronger sense of internal locus of control and so will be more ready to make decisions; many Australians from non-Western backgrounds such as the Indian sub-continent have a much stronger sense of external locus of control and so are more prone to be fatalistic.

Psychologist Alan Roland (2003, p. 277) reflected on over 20 years of experience in treating Indian patients. He comments: "I have found in all my Indian patients, especially those who are Hindus, all of whom are highly educated, usually with graduate degrees, that they assume the presence of a personal destiny that can be fathomed by astrology, palmistry, psychics, the spirit world, dreams, coincidental occurrences, and such, and that can be partially altered by certain rituals."

6.8 Lead for change

Everyone has a critical part to play in the change process of a church that is embracing a new way of 'doing church' that will include those with whom you are not familiar and very likely find interesting as well as challenging. Change has been a part of your whole life and in this sense your journey of becoming more multi-ethnic in your focus will be no different. You and everyone else around you, including those you are intending to embrace as part of your church, will experience mixed emotions and you will find that successes are intermingled with failures.

One way in which individuals can prepare for change is to understand that feelings go through transition when change is introduced. Consider a church in which leaders have made the decision to phase out the playing of an organ during family services. Imagine this is a church in which organ music has always been an integral part of church life and is still much loved, especially by many older members of the church. Typically, there will be a sense of shock at the initial news, followed by denial or disbelief that this is happening and then a sense of anger or disappointment, possibly with some members leaving, before acceptance will have a chance to kick in. Acknowledging feelings of any kind is important if a healthy journey of individual transition is to be achieved.

Decision-makers in the church have a particularly important role to play when making plans and decisions that call for change that will not leave people behind. Consulting with all parties, deciding on what to communicate, and proper timing of communication are some critical matters that must be given careful consideration. Providing channels of feedback, listening actively, gathering and reflecting on the feedback, modifying decisions and plans in the face of feedback, and giving genuine support for people struggling to cope with the change are all important.

Leading for change is not the sole prerogative of staff and formally appointed leaders of the church. Listen to the following true story.

An Anglo Aussie member of a predominantly Anglo Aussie church had a reputation as a prayer warrior. She decided to lead a group of predominantly Chinese members of the church to pray for change in the church in which church members would be less segregated and more deeply engaged with one another across cultures. For the Anglo Aussie member, this required a step of faith and a preparedness to organise and work with a group of people with whom she was not familiar. It was many months before she became an honorary 'Chinese', and now she remains a true friend embraced by the Chinese women she has touched and taught to pray, thanks to her willingness to lead for change.

6.9 Create opportunities to make contact with a variety of people

We are social beings and are made for living in communities. Whatever our personality, history or cultural background, we need one another. God desires that we live in fellowship with one another and the church tries to model this. But community building and living is difficult, and this is seen in the decline of family life in our society. Community building across cultures presents added challenges, given our different histories and backgrounds, values, modes of behaviour and worldviews and perhaps differing socio-economic circumstances. Intentionally reaching out to people in the community will be a challenge for some, but this need not be difficult to do.

Church leaders need to constantly treat key ministries of the church as a means by which its members can connect with the community within and outside of the church. With input from researching the environment in which the church finds itself and by conducting a SWOT analysis, a solid foundation can be laid for some tentative opportunities to be considered. The grapevine is great and should be utilised, but its input should be thoroughly supported by objective data. Consult widely as part of the change program.

What can individuals do to make and strengthen contacts? Start with those around you — your immediate family and then your extended family, followed by friends, neighbours, neighbourhood contacts like the butcher, and work mates. Anecdotally, the average person in Australia is easily in contact with 150 people. Pray that God will direct you to the people with whom you can build relationships and remember to be culturally diverse in your efforts.

A Chinese member of a predominantly Anglo Aussie church took the step of initiating a multi-ethnic hospitality ministry where visitors to the church met to eat and chat in the homes of various church members. Filled with holy boldness, she approached a mix of Chinese and Anglo women to take turns opening up their homes to visitors. At each gathering, consisting of between 6 to 16 visitors, invitations were thought through carefully so that no one culture dominated each gathering. The success of this ministry initiative by one individual from the minority culture contributed greatly to the cross-cultural efforts of the church, not just in terms of the quality of relationships formed but also in terms of some lasting friendships across cultures.

6.10 Develop capabilities to connect with a variety of people

Migrants coming to predominantly Anglo Aussie churches are motivated to befriend the Anglo Aussie communities, as much as they will also try to retain their own minority group connections. When migrants walk away from churches — some after many years of membership and trying to be accepted — the inability to feel a part of the Anglo Aussie community is often cited. This they have often already 'communicated indirectly' in social situations but have not formally articulated until the decision is made to leave the church. Many people will also leave under the pretext of more politically acceptable reasons. Middle Easterners are not dissimilar to Asians in this regard.

Having created opportunities for contact, how are connections made and supported so that genuine relationships can develop? Developing our intrapersonal skills (a close relationship with Jesus, a clear conviction, a strong commitment, resilience, self-care, etc.), interpersonal capabilities (skills, training, etc.) and community resources (mutual relationships, safety, support, etc.) provide the cornerstone for fostering new and ongoing sustainable friendships.

Welcome

Genuine care and love are difficult to practise — pray that God will use us despite our imperfections. There are people we encounter who are ready to give their lives to the Lord because of what God has been doing in their lives before we met them. However, in many instances, people are led to share more of their lives with us when they sense that we love them whether they become Christians or not. Learning to be active listeners who accurately reflect to people what they are communicating to us helps them to sense that we understand them. In time, trust will develop and people will start to share with you what is on their hearts. When you know their issues and what is going on in their lives, you will have the opportunity to pray meaningfully for them and with them and to make Jesus relevant to their lives.

In many cultures that we will encounter, storytelling is a key part of how communication takes place. Learn to tell the gospel in story form and you will have the opportunity to share Jesus in a way that people will understand. Like active listening programs developed by churches and counselling agencies, storytelling the gospel training is also easily accessible in our larger cities.

> An Anglo Aussie professional career woman in suburban Sydney found a new calling in her retirement in reaching out to people of other cultures in her local community. Unused to working amidst a culture that was not predominantly her own, she embarked on some external training as well as some self-learning programs to better equip herself for engaging with members of ethnicities such as Indians and Middle Eastern people. Her minister commented on the ease with which she appeared able to do this and is grateful for the significant contribution she is making to the church.

6.11 Suffer the little children and young adults

We often hear that children and young adults are our future. The absence of children and young adults is usually an indication that a church is not healthy. For obvious reasons, such an absence typically results in churches either becoming irrelevant to their communities or even dying out. The presence of healthy children's and young adults' ministries will greatly help churches to reach out fruitfully to their communities.

The conscious reaching out to ethnic minorities in our community however is very unlikely to be a top priority in the minds of our children and young adults. With some exceptions, which are usually due to parental influence, children are colour-blind to their friends from different ethnic backgrounds Adolescents and young adults on the other hand start to question their identity, including their ethnic and cultural identity, at this time in their lives. Many will struggle with developing their sense of self and so this struggle will also include a questioning of their faith. Some young people may start to consciously embrace reaching out to minorities as an intentional ministry. However, such maturity is rare.

Habits are caught not taught. Parental influences on children's attitudes to other ethnic groups in the community are powerful and they are not always subtle. Some years ago, one of the authors was about to introduce a head of department of a high school to the parent of a Chinese student requiring help with his studies. Upon hearing the Indian name of the teacher, the immediate response of the parent was, "She has dark skin and it will scare my son." It would not be surprising for this child to grow up fearing anyone and everyone who is dark skinned.

Subtle parental influences are even more pervasive. In the majority of our Christian communities, we still see parents choosing to fellowship among their own kind at morning tea after a church service, socialising together with their own kind outside of church, ministering together with their own kind (even when ministering to people from other cultures!), holidaying together with their own kind so that they can relax better, and inviting their own kind to each others' homes. We ought not to be surprised when, as they grow up, our children pick up habits similar to those that we parents practise.

While the onus for involving our children in ministries to other ethnic groups lies largely with the parents, the church has a more direct role to play in relation to involving the young adults. Awareness sessions about who is in our local communities, skill training workshops, local mission activities, and the teaching of the biblical imperative to reach all cultural groups in our community are as important for young adults as they are for older adults. The responsibility for producing the next generation of Christians who will embrace ethnic ministries as a natural part of their loving service of all people lies largely with the church leaders. Short-term mission trips and hands-on cross-cultural 'apprenticeships' within Australia, organised with the help of respected mission agencies, can also play a key role in developing in young people a heart for ministry across cultures.

6.12 Obtain feedback, monitor and evaluate to keep on track

As is the case with all churches, looking after the flock and managing the affairs of a multi-ethnic church is incomplete without having some way of assessing how well it is travelling. If the church is to achieve its goals, what is evaluated and how this is done must be aligned with the vision, mission and aims stated in the strategic plan. It is important to constantly remind church members of what the church is seeking to do and to encourage them by helping them to see how they are contributing to this mission, and to the progress that has been made. When the church's mission plan is clearly kept in mind, it inevitably becomes a major evaluation tool in itself. The greater the commitment of leaders and church members to the mission plan, the keener they will be to avoid wasting resources of effort, time and money on activities and projects that don't contribute to what the church is striving to do.

Evaluating all that is going on in the church against the mission plan also allows leaders to know how well the implementation of the plan is going. While evaluation is conducted periodically, usually quarterly, half yearly and annually, monitoring is keeping an eye on an ongoing basis and may entail short, focused weekly meetings with key colleagues. Monitoring, comparing and giving feedback on how the church is tracking and how each individual is performing in their roles are integral to the evaluation process. Monitoring of activities allows problems to be nipped in the bud. Correct problems as they occur. Feed forward when you anticipate a problem, feed back when a problem occurs for quick correction or further investigation. Honest feedback from trusted colleagues is invaluable and should be welcomed and even sought by all leaders.

A multi-ethnic ministry team was comprised of four Anglo Aussies and five Asian-Australians, the leader being Chinese-Australian. The team began to talk about initiating a home visitation ministry among the Asian members of the church. The leader adopted an *(cont.)*

authoritative stance, allowing only minimal dialogue on the matter and issuing a number of directives to ensure that the project would get off the ground. Immediately after the meeting, two of the Anglo Aussies requested to meet with the leader personally. It transpired that the leader was not even aware of her authoritative manner. The honest feedback from the two Anglo Aussies was given in love and gentleness, and potential conflict arising from this incident was avoided.

To help gauge the fruitfulness of the church's mission, take a careful look at what is being done. To help assess how well the church has been doing the things that are integral to being fruitful, consider carefully what and how things are being done (e.g. prayer, small group ministries, welcoming and hospitality ministries).

6.13 Make sure your administration is appropriate and effective

Administration is often undervalued and underplayed in churches, but it is often in the area of administration that the fruitfulness of a church's ministry is either boosted or undermined. However, administration can soak up a great deal of people's valuable time if not done well. It is often where the rubber hits the road. The way in which churches are administered will convey important messages to the community. A new migrant to the area ringing to get information about the church services can be put off by a loud confident Australian voice at the other end of the phone. Someone seeking emergency childcare may be told that, because this is a church, it is unable to help with childcare, may leave the unintended impression that the church is heartless. A financial contributor to the church, who requires a tax receipt for his donations, is put off when it takes several phone calls and email follow-ups to receive an acknowledgement. Accumulation of such experiences eventually takes a toll on the goodwill of others, no matter how understanding, patient and long-suffering they try to be. Like the effective use of technology, sound financial management tools and engaging volunteers, efficient administration processes and training in effective interpersonal interactions are critical parts of the mission plan of a church.

6.14 Welcome problems and conflicts

Welcome problems — they exist! It is only a matter of whether you are aware of them or not. Be open and encourage people, so that they will approach you with problems. This is also important because leaders are reliant on frontline staff for genuine feedback from church members. See problems as opportunities for growth. Evaluation should be motivating, so it should include positive feedback (techniques such as the sandwich method – positive/point for improvement/positive – of giving feedback are effective). Evaluation should also encourage growth and so include advice and/or suggestions for doing better. Evaluation and feedback to workers should ultimately be empowering. Engage people in problem solving: the more perspectives and input, the greater the volume of information on which to base your informed decisions.

Conflict across cultures is prevalent but often goes unnoticed and/or unacknowledged because of ignorance and/or embarrassment. Such cross-cultural conflict is felt before it is verbalised, so more attention must be given to intuition when working with people from other cultures. Asian-Australians can feel that their concerns have been swept under the carpet when their concerns are aired (sometimes very indirectly) at social occasions and then not taken on board at formal meetings. They struggle to voice their issues at such formal meetings because they want to preserve group harmony and feel that it is not their place to raise problems. If they do, they struggle with how to present their concerns in culturally acceptable ways. Often the concern becomes over-stated and that creates another set of issues to be worked through. By the time they come to a leader with an issue, it is usually at the crisis stage. Socialise extensively to get feedback on how things are going.

Effective ways to resolve conflict are influenced by culture. People from collectivistic cultures are more emotionally expressive about their problems and seek to resolve conflict indirectly. Confrontation is avoided as it causes loss of face. When leaders are providing feedback for change, emphasise the root of the problem externally, without criticising individuals, and suggest what the person can do to change the external factor. In contrast, people from more individualistic cultures treat conflict impersonally and so are more willing to confront differences head-on, armed with facts.

When ministering and working with minority ethnic groups, much more time needs to be spent on empathy than on problem-solving. Further, empathy is expressed differently in different cultures. Western empathy puts one's feelings in the shoes of the other; Asian empathy is expressed as understanding the consequences on one's own image before the community at large. Protect the integrity of Asian friends by protecting their image, to reassure them that their position and work are being protected and appreciated. Stay open to warnings and messages via the expression of emotions related to their integrity.

> A Chinese friend was getting increasingly upset and visibly losing control of her emotions when relating to another friend her frustration and anger with her teenage son, who was going off the rails, not doing well at school and being generally obnoxious at home. The Chinese friend is a high-achiever and was deeply disappointed with her son for not realising his potential and for throwing away all the opportunities she was providing for him to excel academically. In trying to be empathetic, the friend reflected to the Chinese that this must be making her very angry with her son. The Chinese woman immediately denied that she was angry, but said that she was only disappointed. In the Chinese culture, expressions of anger is related to loss of face, and therefore it is not acceptable to express anger publicly. The correct empathetic response in this case is to say 'You are disappointed."

6.15 Go the distance

God determines the time for planting and for harvesting and we as his vessels are called to simply go the distance. Such a commitment is only possible with a clear faith and belief in the work of the Lord that comes from living a prayerful God-centred life. Keeping our eyes on Jesus allows us to weather the ups and downs of 'doing church'. Pray that God will always hold us in his arms to help us on the journey with one undeniable outcome — growth for the Kingdom of God.

For most of us, God has also provided a community of people with different gifts and talents to help us go the distance. These gifts, including money, skills and encouragement, can be utilised to minister to one another in the church as well as to support the work of the church in service and mission to people in the community.

Finally, it is also the responsibility of individuals to look after themselves to the best of their ability. Have a self-care plan and a way of evaluating and keeping yourself accountable. Have a personal development plan so that you may imitate Jesus, keep growing in wisdom and stature and in favour with God and man (Luke 2:52), and be able to go the distance.

6.16 Summary

A faith in the God in whom we believe, and an understanding of who we are and why we do what we do are the start of effective ministry. The more different the culture of your ministry focus group is from your own, the more important it is to be clear about your faith and to cling to it. Faith must then be followed by action, which calls for careful preparation and possibly training to become equipped, sound strategic decisions including those concerned with leadership makeup and key ministry areas, managing change and monitoring progress, effectively handling differences and maintaining personal wellbeing. All these aspects should be integral to the strategic plan of the church that is completely aligned with the vision of "So whether you eat or drink or whatever you do, do it all for the glory of God."

6.17 Questions

1. What strengths do you see in yourself at present that can steer you in your first or next step towards reaching people of other cultures in your local community?

2. What do you currently lack that could assist you in getting started or moving forward in your cross-cultural ministry?

3. What external opportunities do you see in your local community for cross-cultural outreach?

4. What external difficulties do you want to seek help with to enable you to pursue your ideas for cross-cultural work?

5. What are some actions you can take now to ensure your wellbeing so that you can go the distance in your cross-cultural initiatives?

Notes

CONCLUSION

In this book, the authors have briefly taken you on a journey through the WHY, WHAT, HOW and WHEN of reaching Australia's ethnic minorities and developing vibrant churches that are effective in ministering across cultures. The Bible is clear that we are to be gospel carriers to people of all cultures, whether they are found in lands far away, in our neighbourhood or at our doorstep. The authors have shared with you information, data and experiences that they hope challenge Christians in Australia to wake up and reach out to our increasingly multi-ethnic communities in all parts of the country.

The authors are sure that God has been working in your lives as you've undertaken this study. They hope that it has opened your eyes and helped to equip you further to engage with people from a wide range of ethnic backgrounds that might well be very different from your own.

As you follow God's leading into this kind of ministry, the authors recommend that you keep coming back to relevant sections of this book and that you investigate some of the reading and other resources listed in Appendices E and F. The authors are also willing to help your church become more effective in crossing cultures through running workshops and seminars.

You probably have more information and questions to add to the thoughts raised in this book about building churches that can be welcoming homes for people from a variety of cultural backgrounds. Please feel free to contact the authors with any comments or questions you may have, either now or during the course of your cross-cultural ministry. The authors would also appreciate hearing how your ministries are progressing, so that we can learn together from one another's rich experiences. It is amazing what we can learn from each other when we come together in genuine humility with a common purpose — to glorify Jesus.

The authors' shared email address is:

changinglanes.book@gmail.com

MODULE 2

During the three years that preceded his death and resurrection, Jesus ministered almost exclusively to one ethno-religious group, namely Palestinian Jews. Yet, ironically, the Gospels also reveal how Jesus intentionally laid the foundations for an understanding of the People of God that does not involve sharing the same ethnic identity and separating from those who don't share that identity.

1. Consider Jesus' Baptism *(Matthew 3:13-17)*

Only Gentile proselytes were baptised, until John the Baptist came on the scene. By being baptised himself Jesus endorsed the administering of baptism to ethnic Jews as well. This implies that Jewish ethnic identity no longer automatically involves membership in God's people. God's true people are all those, whether ethnically Jewish or not, who receive John's baptism of repentance.

2. Consider Jesus' Identity as 'Son of David, Son of Abraham' *(Matthew 1:1)*

To understand what it means to call Jesus Messiah, the Davidic king, it is necessary, as Matthew's opening genealogy demonstrates, to begin with Abraham. For, as Matthew 2 illustrates, Jesus' identity as 'king of the Jews' is associated with an Abrahamic rule that is of global significance, with Jesus being worshipped by Gentiles, in keeping with the great Abrahamic promises (Genesis 12:1-2). Matthew's Gospel ends with the same emphasis, the absolute rule of Jesus calling for people from all nations to become Jesus' disciples and be incorporated into the people of God.

3. Consider Jesus' disciples' identity as 'the light of the world' (Matthew 5:14)

As Genesis 12:2 indicates, it is through the Abrahamic 'great nation' that God will bring blessing to all peoples. When Jesus called his disciples 'the light of the world' he was applying to them a phrase found in Isaiah. This phrase identifies Jesus' disciples as the great Abrahamic nation of whom God says, "It is too small a thing for you to be my servant to restore the tribes of Jacob and bring back those of Israel I have kept. I will also make you a light for the Gentiles, that my salvation may reach to the ends of the earth" (Isaiah 49:6). Jesus, as 'the Son of David, Son of Abraham', was intent on an extension of the blessings of his rule that was not limited to any particular ethnicity.

MODULE 3

 ACTS 10

This passage reveals how a failure to allow the gospel to transform one's own culture and traditions inhibits Christians from taking the gospel to those who don't share our culture and traditions.

Through this vision God reiterates what Jesus had already effectively declared (see Mark 7:19), namely that all foods are now to be regarded as clean. The fulfilment of the law in Jesus (Matthew 5:17-20) involves a transformation of culture and tradition for Jewish followers of Jesus. Previously the distinction between clean and unclean foods served to shape the Jewish nation as a separate and distinct people, as was God's intent in the preparatory period covered by the Old Testament. But now, following Jesus' life, death and resurrection, there is a radical redefinition of what is meant by membership in the people of God. No longer is it essentially tied to Jewish ethnic identity.

In Acts 10 it is doubtful that there is any insinuation that Peter should already have been doing what God calls him to do via the vision. What happens is not an implicit rebuke of Peter but God's way of helping Jewish Christians to understand how the transformation effected by the gospel necessitates full acceptance of Gentile Christians, without requiring them to adopt traditions still prized by Jewish people. What God revealed through Peter's visionary experience and its dramatic aftermath becomes key evidence in defeating the attempts of some Jewish Christians to regard such traditions as still mandated by God for all God's people, regardless of ethnicity (see Acts 15).

It is significant that Peter was staying in the home of a man who dealt with the skins of dead animals (v6). This indicates that Peter had already taken to heart how the gospel changes the way in which Jews were to think of cleanness and uncleanness. So Peter has entered what strict Jews would have considered an unclean home. Now Peter needs to see the logical extension of this same gospel transformation. If the gospel-effected breakdown of distinctions between cleanness and uncleanness makes it valid to enter the home of an 'unclean' Jew then it also makes it valid to enter the home of an 'unclean' Gentile. As Peter recognises, God has shown him through the vision that he must not call any person impure or unclean (v28).

However, the vision does expose the danger that continued adherence to outdated aspects of culture and tradition holds.

MODULE 4

📖 ACTS 17

Culpable Ignorance and Cultural Intelligence

Cultural intelligence or CQ, as it is often termed, may be simply defined as CQ = "a person's capability to adapt effectively to new cultural contexts."

From what we know of Paul it would appear that he was possessed of considerable cultural intelligence.

Earley & Ang (2003, p. xii) identify three characteristics involved in cultural intelligence:

- Cognition: "Do I know what is happening?"

- Motivation: "Am I motivated to act?"

- Behaviour: "Can I respond appropriately and effectively?"

Paul's speech to the Areopagus is preceded by an account that emphasises his debates with Epicurean and Stoic philosophers in the agora, the marketplace and public forum area. Also underscored is Paul's distress at seeing Athens so full of idols. This is no superficial, knee-jerk emotional response on the part of a narrow-minded religious bigot. As Paul makes clear at the very opening of his Areopagus address, he had made a point of walking around and taking a good look at their objects of worship. All of these cognitive assets, it must be stressed, were not developed as Paul sat at some library desk, poring over books and writing down his summaries and reflections. Rather, his ability to understand the different cultural environs in which he found himself was developed in the context of constant cross-cultural interaction with people.

So, then, Paul possessed the first characteristic of CQ. His ability to adapt effectively to the Athenian cultural context was grounded in a remarkable cognitive ability to understand what was happening in Athenian culture.

There is no doubting Paul's motivation. In the first place, his dismay at seeing the scale of idolatry in Athens motivated him to engage with people. He had a wonderful gospel message to communicate and his assessment of Athenian religion and culture underlined the Athenians' need to hear that message. Paul was clearly sensitive to his need to communicate this message in a manner that took into account the cultural, religious and philosophical distinctives of the people of Athens. Paul was motivated to adapt to this new cultural context.

Thirdly, Paul demonstrated through what he did and said that he knew how to adapt in an appropriate and effective manner. Of course, the central challenge that his message involved — submission to Jesus as the living Lord who rose from the dead — was alien to the cultural and religious world in which the Athenians had been acculturated. Nevertheless, Paul showed considerable skill in the way he interacted with his audience about Greek literature and philosophy, so as to communicate his message in a way which struck home powerfully to at least some of his audience.

Paul, then, presents us with a fine model of cultural intelligence. But it is important not to make the mistake of construing Paul's extraordinary cultural sensitivity as involving downplaying or even sidestepping the essential gospel in his endeavour to find common ground. Some have even described Paul's speech as an instance of pre-evangelism.

First of all, we must recognise Paul's speech as a valid presentation of the gospel. Luke does not give us the full text of Paul's address, only a summary of it. However, the speech concludes in a standard call for repentance and with an emphasis upon the resurrection of Jesus and its implications. The book of Acts is emphatic that the gospel centres on witnessing to the resurrection of Jesus and indeed in verse 18 we discover that, prior to his speech at the Areopagus, Paul had been communicating this same gospel.

Secondly, it is precarious to see Paul as going out of his way to accommodate his presentation of the gospel to the cultural context in which he found himself. What we can say is that there were elements of his presentation of the gospel to Jews which Paul did not find it necessary to highlight in his communication of the gospel to unbelieving Gentiles.

The following list indicates those elements which Paul included in his presentation of the gospel to Jews:

1. Jesus as the Son of God and Messiah (Acts 9:20, 22; 13:23; 17:3)

2. Jesus as the Saviour of Israel (i.e., being Messiah; Acts 13:23)

3. Election of Israel (Acts 13:17)

4. Review of Jewish history (Acts 13:17ff)

5. Importance of John the Baptist (Acts 13:24-25)

6. Jewish failure to recognise Jesus and their guilt in effecting his death (Acts 13:27-29)

7. The biblical (OT) necessity of the death and resurrection of the Messiah (Acts 17:2-3)

8. The death and burial of Jesus (Acts 13:28-29)

9. The resurrection of Jesus by God (Acts 13:30)

10. Witnesses to Jesus' resurrection (Acts 13:31; 22:15)

11. Paul's own witnessing of Jesus as the Risen Lord (Acts 22:6-10, 22:15)

12. Jesus' resurrection as the fulfilment of God's promise and purpose (Acts 13:32-37)

13. The citation of Old Testament Scripture now fulfilled in Christ (Acts 13:33-37)

14. Jesus' superiority to David (Acts 13:36-37)

15. Forgiveness for Jews through Jesus (Acts 13:38)

16. Inability of the Law of Moses to justify Jews (Acts 13:39)

17. Warning against tragic consequences of unbelief and rejection of the gospel (Acts 13:40-41)

18. The necessity to proclaim the gospel to Jews first (Acts 13:46)

19. The call to preach the gospel to Gentiles, in fulfilment of Scripture (Acts 13:46-47)

20. Paul's own pedigree as a Jew (Acts 22:2-5)

21. Paul's conversion (Acts 22:6ff)

Many of these elements are conspicuous for their absence in Paul's communication of the gospel to the Gentiles. We can certainly say that cultural considerations affect profoundly the content of what Paul has to say. Paul does not need to rehearse Jewish history and their rejection of Christ. Paul does not speak of the Law of Moses. Paul does not cite Old Testament Scriptures and seek to show their fulfilment in Christ. He does not seek to prove that Jesus is the Messiah.

These considerations have practical significance. There are some standardised Western methods of sharing the gospel, e.g., Evangelism Explosion, Two Ways to Live, The Bridge Illustration, etc. It cannot be assumed that these methods transfer into other cultural settings. In certain cultural contexts the entire method may have to be ditched and a completely different mode of presentation be developed. In many cultural contexts the content of the method concerned may have to be drastically modified. The authors' experience has been that in most instances modification of such standardised methods to allow for cultural differences has been grossly inadequate.

MODULE 5

 **GALATIANS 2**

"When in Rome Do What the Romans Do"?

In Galatians 2 Paul provides us with two settings:

1. What happened when he took a Gentile with him to Jerusalem (v1-10)?

2. What happened when the Jewish Peter was in Antioch (v11-13)?

When in Jerusalem it was not a case of "When in Jerusalem do what the Jerusalemites do," for it was not appropriate for Titus to be circumcised.

When in Antioch it was a case of "When in Antioch do what the Antiocheans do," for it was right for Peter to eat with Gentiles.

Galatians does not teach us, "When in Rome do what the Romans do," for Galatians 2 illustrates for Christians that the issue is not one of cultural relativism but of loyalty to the gospel. The principle is "When in Rome do what the gospel would have you do."

First, look at verses 1-10 concerning what happened when Paul took with him to Jerusalem a Gentile named Titus. He tells us, "I went in response to a revelation and, meeting privately with those esteemed as leaders, I presented to them the gospel that I preach among the Gentiles." (v2a). Paul wanted to make sure, as he puts it, that he wasn't "running or had been running (his) race in vain" (v2b). He knows that all Christians had a particularly high regard for Jesus' apostles and James, Jesus' brother, the leaders of the church in Jerusalem. Paul wants to clarify whether there was any essential difference in the gospel preached by the leaders of the Jerusalem church and the gospel he himself was communicating.

It is important to understand how Paul thought about the leaders in Jerusalem. The words "who seemed to be leaders" indicates that Paul places a limit on their authority and this is confirmed by other comments Paul makes about these same leaders in this passage. So, in verse 6 he says, "As for those who seemed to be important — whatever they were makes no difference to me; God does not judge by external appearances..." Again in verse 9 he speaks of "James, Peter and John, those reputed to be pillars." So every time Paul speaks of the authority of these leaders he adds either the phrase "who seemed to be" or "those reputed."

H.L. Mencken (1956, p. 13) once quipped, "We must respect the other fellow's religion, but only in the sense and to the extent that we respect his theory that his wife is beautiful and his children smart." It is wrong to think that Paul is expressing disdain or disrespect for these leaders and what they think. He is simply indicating that the authority of these leaders does not depend on what Christians think about them but on how God, "who does not judge by external appearance", thinks about them.

Paul had an immense intellect and a far more extensive education than any of the church of Jerusalem leaders. However, notwithstanding Paul's brilliance, he accepts that if there is an essential difference between the message he communicates and that proclaimed by the leaders in Jerusalem, then this might indicate he himself had got it all wrong, as he tells us in verse 2: "I went in response to a revelation and, meeting privately with those esteemed as leaders, I presented to them the gospel that I preach among the Gentiles. I wanted to be sure I was not running and had not been running my race in vain."

This trip to Jerusalem was very encouraging. The leaders of the church in Jerusalem and Paul were all reading from the same page; they were all committed to preaching the same gospel. Paul cites as the first evidence of this: "Yet not even Titus, who was with me, was compelled to be circumcised, even though he was a Greek" (v3). The proof of the pudding is in the eating. When Paul preached the gospel to Gentiles he did not require them to get circumcised either before or after they placed their faith in Christ. The leaders of the church in Jerusalem similarly recognise that Christian Jews must part company from non-Christian Jews on this matter.

We began with the quote: "When in Rome do what the Romans do." These words go back to something that happened in AD 387, when Augustine arrived in Milan. The Church in Milan didn't do things the same way as the Church in Rome. In Rome it was the custom for Christians to fast on Saturday. In Milan Christians didn't do this. Augustine wasn't sure what to do, so he asked the Bishop of Milan, Ambrose. Ambrose explained, "When I am at Rome, I fast on a Saturday; when I am at Milan, I do not. Follow the custom of the Church where you are."

We may be a little unfair to Ambrose, but this statement does illustrate where the early church started to go wrong. While at one level his advice seems sensible, it is also disturbing because Ambrose is proposing that "the custom of the Church," that is, church tradition, albeit local church tradition, should be the fundamental criterion used by Christians to decide how they should conduct themselves. But this, of course, is precisely what does not happen when Paul takes Titus to Jerusalem. They do not follow the custom of the Church of Jerusalem and that is precisely the point of the passage, because it is the gospel and not Jewish Christian culture or local church tradition which must determine Christian conduct.

It should now be apparent from what happened in Jerusalem that for Christians the principle is not "When in Rome do what the Romans do," but "When in Rome do what the Romans do if it doesn't compromise the gospel." The principle is not "When in Rome do what the church in Rome does," but "When in Rome do what the church in Rome does if it doesn't compromise the gospel." Christians are called to be culturally sensitive but we are not called to be cultural chameleons.

Paul views Peter as his counterpart since Peter had been given the task of preaching the gospel to the Jews, just as Paul had been given the task of preaching the gospel to the Gentiles (v7). When Peter first goes to Antioch he acts in a manner which is a natural extension of how he and the other leaders treated Titus in Jerusalem. Before the coming of Jesus Christ the Jews had always insisted that any Gentiles who wanted to become part of God's people must submit to the same requirements of Old Testament law they themselves accepted — circumcision, food laws and observance of the Jewish religious calendar. But the leaders of the church in Jerusalem, including Peter, accept Titus as a Christian brother, as a fully-fledged member of God's people, without placing any pressure on him to be circumcised. Consistent with this, when Peter comes to Antioch he "used to eat with the Gentiles" (v12b).

A key phrase used in verses 1-10 recurs in verses 11-21 — "the truth of the gospel" (vv5, 15). When Paul was in Jerusalem he was determined to ensure that "the truth of the gospel" was preserved for Gentile Christians. When Peter first came to Antioch he was "acting in line with the truth of the gospel" when, ignoring Jewish food laws and caveats against eating with the uncircumcised, he entered Gentile homes and ate with them. But in verse 14 Paul is observing that Peter and the other Jewish Christians in Antioch were no longer "acting in line with the truth of the gospel."

What went wrong? Again note how Paul skilfully draws a contrast between what happened in Jerusalem and what happened in Antioch. Look at verse 4: "This matter arose (the matter of whether Titus, a Gentile, should be circumcised or not) because some false believers had infiltrated our ranks to spy on the freedom we have in Christ Jesus and to make us slaves." Now look at why things went wrong in Antioch: "For before certain men came from James, he (Peter) used to eat with the Gentiles. But when they arrived, he began to draw back and separate himself from the Gentiles because he was afraid of those who belonged to the circumcision group" (v12). Richard Baxter noted, "Dangers bring fears, and fears more dangers bring." That's what happens here. Since Peter was the tallest poppy in Christendom his actions were in grave danger of creating a permanent rift between Jewish and Gentile Christians.

In verse 4 Paul describes these people who insist that Titus be circumcised as 'false believer', that is, people who falsely believed they were Christians. You can live in a garage but that doesn't make you a car. You can make noises like a car but it still doesn't make you a car. There are many today who, like these 'false brothers', attend church and deceive themselves when they profess to be Christians.

When Titus was in Jerusalem Peter and the other leaders backed Paul to the hilt and they unitedly defended the truth of the gospel. But now when Peter is on his own in Antioch he becomes "afraid of those who belonged to the circumcision group." His fear now causes him to take circumcision and therefore the Jewish law as constituting an essential difference between Jewish Christians and Gentile Christians. His fear of these intimidating and highly aggressive false Christians causes him to say to the Gentile Christians in Antioch, "I can no longer eat with you because you are uncircumcised and don't practise Jewish food laws."

Consequently Paul publicly confronts Peter. There is a story about two men living in a small village who got into a terrible dispute. The first man went to the home of the local sage and told his version of what happened. When he finished, the sage said, "You're absolutely right." The next night, the second man called on the sage and told his side of the story. The sage responded, "You're absolutely right." Afterward, the sage's wife scolded her husband. "Those men told you two different stories and you told them they were absolutely right. That's impossible — they can't both be absolutely right." The sage turned to his wife and said, "You're absolutely right."

Many people think it is sage to avoid conflict. We laugh at the sage's response to his wife, but she is correct: "they can't both be absolutely right." Indeed, Paul is faced with a situation where Peter is 'absolutely wrong' in what he has done. Paul recalls, "When Peter came to Antioch, I opposed him to his face, because he was in the wrong." Peter is clearly departing from the way in which he and the other leaders had acted when Paul took Titus to Jerusalem. Peter was clearly out of step with what they had all agreed upon at that time regarding "the truth of the gospel."

Notice how Paul begins his open rebuke of Peter. In verse 14 Paul says, "When I saw that they were not acting in line with the truth of the gospel, I said to Cephas in front of them all, 'You are a Jew, yet you live like a Gentile and not like a Jew. How is it, then, that you force Gentiles to follow Jewish customs?'" When Titus was in Jerusalem the circumcision party, the legalistic false Christians, tried to force Titus to follow Jewish customs and failed. Now Peter, afraid of the circumcision party, is himself "(forcing) Gentiles to follow Jewish customs." In verse 13 Paul speaks of Peter's 'hypocrisy', here using a word that belongs to the world of Greek theatre and means essentially 'play-actor'. In other words, Peter, and the other Jewish Christians, are putting on a pathetic performance to please the aggressive members of the circumcision party. As Paul reminds him, Peter, though a Jew, no longer privately observes Jewish food laws. But Peter wants to avoid conflict; he wants to avoid trouble, so for the sake of keeping the peace he puts on a public show of being a good, observant Jew.

In verses 15-21 Paul magnificently reminds Peter of the gospel they both had agreed on when Paul was in Jerusalem. By his actions Peter is communicating a wrong gospel. Peter was sounding out a doleful dirge, making it seem as though only those Christians are rightly regarded by God (justified) who observe the Jewish law, especially circumcision and Jewish food laws. The crescendo of Paul's great gospel symphony is scaled in verse 21, "I do not set aside the grace of God, for if righteousness could be gained through the law, Christ died for nothing." To treat obedience to the Jewish law as essential to the way one will be viewed by God is to "set aside the grace of God," since God is not impressed by anything we do even if it involves obeying things he commanded. To treat obedience to the Jewish law as essential to the way one stands before God is also to say in effect: "Christ died for nothing," because, as Paul reminds Peter, in the process of seeking the right standing with God which is only to be found in Christ, Jews like them discover they themselves are sinners (v17) whose only hope is the death of Christ and not anything they are personally able to achieve through compliance with Old Testament requirements.

We have learnt to treat with caution the popular maxim "When in Rome do what the Romans do." We do need to be culturally sensitive and flexible as Peter was when he first came to Antioch and ate with Gentiles in their homes. But, first and foremost, we must have a clear understanding of the gospel and refuse to allow any culture to compromise its truth. So, for example, it would have been wrong to have pressured Titus, a Gentile, to be circumcised and it was very wrong when Peter allowed his own Jewish culture to make him treat Gentiles as second class citizens.

MODULE 6

ACTS 10:9-29

Christian leaders who are trying to implement significant change in their churches will find that church members vary greatly in their attitude towards change. There are:

1. **Innovators:** These are people who like change and indeed often initiate it. They pose some dangers. Firstly, they may want change to occur

at a speed the rest of church is not ready for. Secondly, their own strong personal involvement in change may create the perception that change is their idea, not that of church members more generally.

2. **Early Adopters:** Such people are more numerous than the innovators. Among the early adopters are people with influence. If they desire change then it is best to let such people be the ones to persuade others.

3. **Early Majority:** These folk are ready to be persuaded by Early Adopters. The way change is handled with these church members is critical. When they accept that it is right to change then it is urgent that change be implemented and not left hanging. Otherwise, the enthusiasm of such church members may transmute into frustration, accompanied by criticism of leadership for undue slowness in effecting change.

4. **Late Majority:** These folk are often persuaded during the process of change itself. Such church members are ready to adjust once they see change is inevitable and, more importantly, that it is what the majority wants.

5. **Laggards:** There are some who will probably remain opposed to the change. Such members are always ready to say things were better before the change. Since there will almost always be such people, it is a mistake to delay change until there is unanimity — something that leads to greater overall discontent (adapted from Heywood, 2003, p. 3).

Case Study: There was a pinkeye epidemic among the Motilones, a tribal group of Indians in a remote Colombian jungle area. The traditional healer ('witch doctor') had been unable to bring healing through her incantations, potions and prayers. Missionary Bruce Olson offered her the antibiotic Terramycin as a possible cure. She rejected it, saying, "You are white. Your ways are different from ours."

Olson had decided there was no demonic element in her *(cont.)*

traditional healing practices. So when he himself contracted pinkeye he asked her for help. She tried unsuccessfully to heal him. When Olson returned, clearly unhealed, he asked her to perform her incantations again but this time to put Terramycin in his eyes as well. She agreed and three days later he became the first person to be healed. Olson commended her for healing him with Terramycin and suggested she might be able to do this with her people as well. Within three days everyone in the tribe was cured.

Later the traditional healer introduced disinfectants into tribal ceremonies and other health measures. Eventually, health centres were established among this tribal group, administered and staffed by Motilones (adapted from Elmer, 1993, pp. 60-61).

The following principles may be derived from the Motilone Case Study (modified from Elmer):

1. Relationships. Whenever possible, choose friendship over confrontation. Romans 12:18: "If it is possible, as far as it depends on you, live at peace with everyone." Olson could have directly healed the tribespeople, while shaming and alienating the traditional healer. He acted wisely so as to still bring about healing for the tribespeople, while also befriending the traditional healer.

2. Resources. Use the church's own ways, methods, facilities, and people in the introduction of change as often as possible. Olson allowed the traditional healer to try her methods of healing on him, using this as the way in which to introduce the cure for pinkeye. Disinfectant was introduced via the traditional healer into tribal ceremonies. Motilone tribespeople became the administrators and staff for the later medical centres.

3. Roles. Introduce change in such a way that it does not violate the patterns and roles of people who are well placed to facilitate change. Olson was careful to respect the role of the traditional healer and to effect change in a way that brought honour to her from tribespeople, while giving her the satisfaction of actually being involved in bringing

healing to her people.

4. Relevance. Introduce change in a way that is relevant to church members. Build upon what is known and practised. Not only was disinfectant introduced via tribal ceremonies, but vaccination was also introduced as another form of traditional bloodletting.

5. Responsibility. Ensure that sustaining the change does not depend upon the presence of an outsider. Once Olson had got the traditional healer to use Terramycin to cure him, she herself administered it to her tribespeople.

6. Reliance. Keep central the role of the Holy Spirit, for "without Him there would have been no real or lasting development" (Olson). Fundamental to God-honouring change are right attitudes: "But I say, walk by the Spirit, and you will not gratify the desires of the flesh. For the desires of the flesh are against the Spirit, and the desires of the Spirit are against the flesh, for these are opposed to each other, to keep you from doing the things you want to do" (Galatians 5:16-17).

Considerations (adapted from Heywood, 2003, pp. 3-4):

1. Listen. People must know their opinions have been heard and valued. If this is so, such people may reconcile to change, despite some uncertainty.

2. Explain. Explain the problem(s) and reasons for the plan being adopted over and over again to an ever-widening group of people. Don't assume people understand the first time they hear this.

3. Value criticism. This helps to sharpen planning and uncover unforeseen problems.

4. Recognise the disadvantages of the proposed change and be open about them. This better prepares people.

5. Work in the negative force field. "The overall drive of the congregation

is a balance between the positive energy of those in favour of the change and the negative energy of those opposing it" (Heywood 2003, p. 4). Negative drive is reduced as opponents feel their point of view and concerns about the change have been recognised and respected.

6. Courtesy. Don't rush the change, rubbish objections, use spiritual blackmail ("this change is the Lord's will"), become too personally involved, break the rules, bring changes behind people's backs or otherwise disregard established consultation procedures.

"A state without some means of change is without the means of its conservation" - Edmund Burke (as cited in Bullard 2011, p. 167).

"Change is not made without inconvenience, even from worst to better" - Samuel Johnson

Dentist before a procedure: "This may hurt!"

APPENDIX B: FACING THE DEMOGRAPHIC REALITY

If you walk around Fairfield in Sydney's west today, you might find it difficult to believe that not so long ago this was a fairly typical Australian big-city suburb, mostly made up of Anglo Aussies working in a range of occupations and spending weekends running kids to Saturday morning sport, having barbecues or watching TV, with a good proportion attending churches on Sundays.

But much of that has changed. As of 2016, this is one of Sydney's most multi-ethnic suburbs. More than half of the residents were born overseas, mostly in non-English speaking countries. The majority of residents speak a language other than English at home, with the two most common ones being Arabic and Assyrian Neo-Aramaic. There are also many Vietnamese migrants and Vietnamese Australians. Some of the churches have closed down as the Anglo Aussie residents have re-located to more Anglo Aussie localities, with the new Fairfield residents not replacing them in church.

Fairfield is now typical of many of the suburbs in our larger cities right around the country. Not only is there a vast range of ethnic backgrounds reflected in the profile of these suburbs, but the faith backgrounds are often very different from what used to be the case. Often, people from a traditionally Christian background make up a very small percentage of the residents, leading to shrinking, dying, amalgamated or closed churches where the new challenges have not been addressed. Some of the church buildings have now been taken over as shops or places of worship for other faiths.

Change in our demography is not a sudden development. Australia has had waves of migrants arrive over many decades, but these were mainly so-called 'white' immigrants from European, and traditionally Christian, backgrounds. They included people born in the UK, Italy and Greece. Census figures in the 1970s and 80s reveal that the majority were from the UK and Southern Europe. They were often referred to as 'new Australians'.

What has changed more recently is the significant increase in new settlers from Asian, Middle Eastern and African regions over the past 20 or so years and many of these people have non-Christian belief systems. We are now all living in a new Australia, with different challenges and opportunities for Christians.

It is helpful for churches to understand the demographics of the community in which they are placed. This does not presuppose that the composition of churches should reflect their communities. Some would contend for this, but this is a controversial matter. We certainly would not want the nature of the community to determine the nature of the church. We certainly do want to recognise that ultimately only God determines who in our community will be redeemed. But with such qualifications, a church is clearly acting in a responsible manner when, with gospel-focused intent, it seeks as best it can to understand those to whom the Lord has led them. Besides, many churches will see it as part of their charter to contribute to the wellbeing of the communities in which they are located. Demographic information will not tell a church all that may be good to know about the community. However, the ready availability of considerable demographic data in Australia is a resource we would be unwise to neglect.

The authors can't possibly present demographic data for each community relevant to every church in Australia. In what follows they are simply presenting broad brush-strokes. This particular section is deliberately not included as a module precisely because the data that follows will soon become dated. It will be up to your church to update such information.

Consider Table 4. It shows that, even in the past 10 years, the number of people living in Australia but born abroad has increased considerably. The increases are largest in our capital and larger regional cities, as you'd expect, since this is where jobs are most likely to be found. Right now, more than 3 people in 10 around our vast country were born overseas. In Melbourne, Perth and Sydney, this figure is closer to 4 in 10. Anglicare research, which built on the work of eminent demographer Charles Price, indicated that by 2025 around half of Sydney's population would be from non-Anglo Aussie backgrounds.

171

Table 3: *Country of birth and language spoken at home by census year*

	Born in Australia (%)			Speak a language other than English at home* (%)		
	2001	**2006**	**2011**	**2001**	**2006**	**2011**
Canberra	77.3	77.1	74.7	15.1	15.2	18.9
Adelaide	75.3	74.9	73.5	10.1	15.9	18.0
Brisbane	78.0	76.8	74.0	13.4	11.3	13.9
Darwin	79.1	79.5	75.7	14.2	14.0	17.8
Hobart	87.7	87.2	86.1	4.8	5.3	6.7
Melbourne	69.8	69.0	66.8	26.9	27.9	30.5
Perth	66.8	66.3	63.3	14.2	14.8	17.6
Sydney	66.6	65.5	63.6	29.2	31.4	34.3
All Australia	76.9	76.1	73.9	16.0	16.8	19.2

*This may be in addition to English

Source: Australian Bureau of Statistics
All figures are based on Place of Usual Residence (PUR) data
All 2001 and 2006 figures for cities are based on Statistical Division (SD) data
All 2011 figures for cities are based on Greater Capital City Statistical Area (GCCSA) data except for Canberra, which is based on Canberra–Queanbeyan (Canberra Part UCL 802001) data
Figures are based on those who answered the relevant census question, not the total number of people interviewed

Figure 3: Country of birth and language spoken at home by census year for all Australia (%)

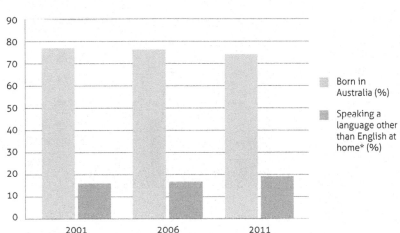

*This may be in addition to English

Source: Australian Bureau of Statistics
All figures are based on Place of Usual Residence (PUR) data
Figures are based on those who answered the relevant census question, not
the total number of people interviewed

Another interesting observation is that the countries where re-settlers were born are no longer predominantly European. In the 2011 national census, people born in mainland China overtook for the first time those born in Italy or Greece (Figure 4).

The 2011 Census revealed that in the Sydney suburb of Fairfield only 19.0% spoke English as their first language. 15.0% spoke Arabic, 18.6% Assyrian, 10.9% Vietnamese, 4.6% Spanish and 3.1% Mandarin.

In Punchbowl only 21.3% spoke English as their first language. 41.7% spoke Arabic, 8.2% Vietnamese, 5.5% Greek, 3.6% Cantonese and 2.3% Indonesian.

(Source: Australian Bureau of Statistics [State Suburb data])

Figure 4: Numbers of people born outside Australia by census year, by country of birth

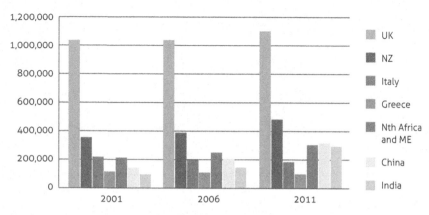

Source: Australian Bureau of Statistics
All figures are based on Place of Usual Residence (PUR) data

The 2011 Census shows that in Queensland, Brisbane has the highest proportion of foreign-born residents, followed by the Gold Coast and Logan. In six Brisbane suburbs — Robertson, Stretton, Macgregor, Sunnybank, Calamvale and Runcorn — more than half of all residents were born overseas. Those born overseas account for more than 40% of the population in a further 13 Brisbane suburbs.

Figure 5 shows the top ten most commonly spoken non-English languages from the 2011 census, with the number of Mandarin speakers overtaking speakers of Italian and Greek for the first time, and Arabic speakers outnumbering Greek speakers.

Figure 5: Top ten languages other than English spoken in Australia

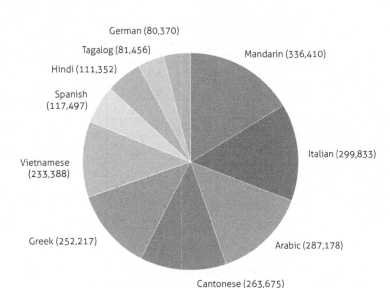

German (80,370)
Tagalog (81,456)
Hindi (111,352)
Spanish (117,497)
Mandarin (336,410)
Italian (299,833)
Vietnamese (233,388)
Greek (252,217)
Arabic (287,178)
Cantonese (263,675)

Source: Australian Bureau of Statistics 2011 Census
All figures are based on Place of Usual Residence (PUR) data

Table 4 shows the religious affiliation of people living in our capital cities, as well as national figures. Whilst percentages of people from Buddhist, Hindu and Muslim backgrounds total just less than 6% of our population in the latest census figures (the 2011 census), this figure has grown from less than 4% in 2001 and about 4.5% in 2006. This represents an increase of about 52% since 2001 and about 30% since 2006. Christians need to be aware of these dramatic changes in our environment. They need to prepare and equip themselves to reach out and engage cross-culturally, which will often be to people very receptive to the gospel of Jesus.

Table 4: Religious affiliation by census year (%)

	Buddhism			Hinduism			Islam		
	2001	2006	2011	2001	2006	2011	2001	2006	2011
Canberra	2.3	2.5	2.8	0.8	1.1	1.8	1.2	1.5	2.3
Adelaide	1.9	2.2	2.4	0.2	0.5	1.2	0.7	1.0	1.6
Brisbane	1.8	2.0	2.2	0.5	0.7	1.1	0.7	0.9	1.3
Darwin	2.5	2.6	2.9	0.4	0.5	1.3	0.9	1.0	1.3
Hobart	0.7	0.8	0.9	0.2	0.3	0.5	0.3	0.3	0.6
Melbourne	3.5	3.9	4.3	0.8	1.3	2.2	2.9	3.2	3.9
Perth	2.3	2.5	2.7	0.4	0.6	1.3	1.5	1.7	2.3
Sydney	3.8	4.2	4.4	1.3	1.9	2.8	3.7	4.4	5.1
All Australia	2.1	2.4	2.7	0.6	0.8	1.4	1.7	1.9	2.4

Source: Australian Bureau of Statistics
All figures are based on Place of Usual Residence (PUR) data
All 2001 and 2006 figures for cities are based on Statistical Division (SD) data
All 2011 figures for cities are based on Greater Capital City Statistical Area (GCCSA) data except for Canberra, which is based on Canberra–Queanbeyan (Canberra Part UCL 802001) data
Figures are based on those who answered the relevant census question, not the total number of people interviewed

Figure 6: Growth in the followers of most common non-Christian religions

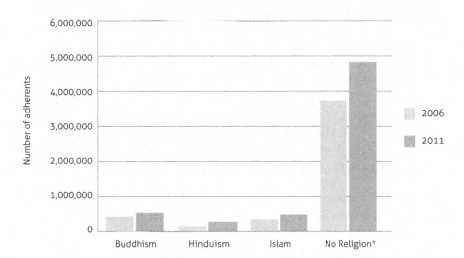

* 'No religion' includes no religion, agnosticism, atheism, humanism and rationalism

Source: Australian Bureau of Statistics

All figures are based on Place of Usual Residence (PUR) data

In some parts of Australia there are particularly high proportions of non-Christian religionists. In 2011 in Greater Dandenong, for example, 17.6% of the population were Buddhists, 10.8% Muslims and 12.9% marked themselves down as having no religion (LGA 22670).

This is more noticeable in our capital cities, where some suburbs have more than 70% of their residents speaking another language besides English. They are also being observed in some of our larger regional centres, especially as the government encourages people to move to these centres, or locates refugees from Africa, the Middle East and South Asia there. Recently, one of the authors took a road trip from Sydney to Adelaide and was interested to be served in a country town fast-food restaurant by a woman wearing a hijab.

The significant numbers of people who don't speak English well in our cities and many regional centres provide great opportunities for churches to provide ESL (English as a Second Language) classes and Easy English Bible Study groups and/or church services.

In the 2011 census, about 23% of Wollongong's population (Statistical Area 3) was born overseas (and 17% speak a language other than English at home), and the same is true of Ipswich (23%) (SA4). For Geelong, this figure is around 17% (11% speaking a language other than English) (SA3)and for Launceston, 12% (6%) (SA3). In Western Australia, 20% of Bunbury's (6%) and 26% of Mandurah's (5%) populations are overseas-born (SA3). So, increasingly, there are little-reached people groups living right within many of our neighbourhoods, if we have the eyes to see them.

However, our churches don't reflect this demographic. As already mentioned, the authors are not saying that they necessarily should, but this is a concern to the extent that it may indicate a widespread lack of effort on the part of churches to reach non-Christians from whatever ethnic or cultural background they may come. We would certainly hope to see many churches far more reflective of their communities than they actually are.

For example, consider the church one of the authors attends. Imagine that it was the clearly communicated vision of the church to be reflective of its community. If so, then if the church were effectively reaching out to minorities in the community, there would be several more from Eastern European backgrounds in the congregation, but there are not. There would be more of Chinese ethnicity and some from the Indian sub-continent. It could be said that those groups have their own churches to attend, but that's frequently not the case. Often, they have very little to do with Christians in the course of their daily lives. And we are all the poorer, as we have so much to learn from people of ethnic and faith backgrounds different from our own.

There is no indication at present that these kinds of trends will stop anytime soon. In fact, with an increasingly globalised world, and with growing involuntary movements of refugees fleeing from difficult situations, Australia may well become home to an increasing percentage of people from other nations around our world. And the 'new Australians' we're seeing are now usually not just from Anglo or European backgrounds, but from scores of other countries in Asia, Africa and the Middle East.

As we're all well aware, this leads to a range of responses in Australia's existing population. Some people are worried — what will this influx mean and what will become of Australia's culture? Some feel it can only be good for the country. Others are happy as long as 'they' don't interfere with their own lifestyles. But what are the implications for the church? How should Christians respond to a very different ethnic and religious profile right in our neighbourhoods and towns?

Note that the statistics shown in this module are largely taken from data provided by the Australian Bureau of Statistics, which conducts a nation-wide census every five years. Most of the data quoted are from the 2001, 2006 and 2011 censuses. Obviously, with the passage of time, these data will become obsolete and the reader should consult more recent figures.

You can refer to the Australian Bureau of Statistics' excellent website, at www.abs.gov.au. It is updated regularly. You can also obtain demographic data for your own suburb or town by going to your local government website. Most of these local government sites will have a 'Community Profile' link that will provide just what you need to find out who lives near your church.

Another excellent resource is the data provided by the National Church Life Survey (NCLS). NCLS research (info@ncls.org.au, www.ncls.org.au) can provide resources written for churches to examine government census figures. Useful materials include profiles centred on the exact address of a church or potential church plant, key maps for selected groups, highlights of important changes, and a workbook for church leaders to explore the figures and plan for the future.

APPENDIX C: EVALUATING WHERE YOU ARE IN YOUR CROSS-CULTURAL CAPABILITIES

Instructions

1. Tick those questions that are relevant to you personally.

2. Answer the questions that you have ticked.

3. Highlight the 'Yes' answers.

4. Decide if there is one initiative among the 'Yes' answers that you can take to start this ministry.

5. Commit to a time for getting started.

6. Seek help, first from within your church (church members own this ministry and often there are hidden talents waiting to be used).

7. Additional help can also be sourced from churches in the denomination to which you belong.

8. Check out the resources and literature to read in Appendices E and F.

For the early stages of establishing cross-cultural ministry

Question	Yes	No	Maybe
1. Can you state the first step your church should make to develop ministry across cultures?	○	○	○
2. Do you know how your church can go about identifying and assessing the strategies for ministry across cultures that are most appropriate for your community?	○	○	○
3. Can you determine which people group or groups your church can specifically engage for ministry?	○	○	○

Question	Yes	No	Maybe
4. Do you know how your church can go about planting a church among a particular ethnic group?	◯	◯	◯
5. Can you work out what kind of model is most suitable for your church in developing multi-ethnic ministry?	◯	◯	◯
6. Do the leaders of your church have a particular conviction as to what kind of church model or range of models is mandated by the Bible?	◯	◯	◯
7. Do you know how your church can go about developing a cross-cultural ministry when there are not yet many people of minority backgrounds in the church's vicinity?	◯	◯	◯
8. Do you know how to go about understanding the specific needs of ethnic minorities in your particular community and ways you can assess the effectiveness of your outreach efforts to them?	◯	◯	◯
9. Do you know where your church can get competent advice in deciding how to begin or develop such a ministry?	◯	◯	◯

For pastors, leaders and denominations in particular

	Yes	No	Maybe
10. Where the leaders of a church are in earnest about developing ministry across cultures, do you know how church members who are used to a long-established model of church can be helped to see the need of the church to reach out to people cross-culturally?	◯	◯	◯
11. Do you know how you can encourage your church members to become sensitive and open to church members of different cultures?	◯	◯	◯
12. Do you know how leaders can respond to obstructive attitudes, including racial prejudice, expressed by members of the church?	◯	◯	◯

Question	Yes	No	Maybe
13. Can you develop a culturally relevant pastoral ministry among members of the congregation that includes addressing the needs of people from differing ethnic and cultural backgrounds?	○	○	○
14. Do you know how pastors and leaders should respond and act when a church member or group of church members express their desire to commence a multi-ethnic ministry of some kind?	○	○	○
15. Can you make sure that they receive support and encouragement commensurate with other supported church ministries?	○	○	○
16. Do you know how your church can provide suitable training (conceptual and experiential) to equip leaders and laity for ministry across cultures?	○	○	○
17. Do you know how leadership structures can be developed which are not dominated by the majority culture of church members?	○	○	○
18. When leadership meetings that have good representation of minority groups are convened, do you know what format these meetings should take so that they are not dominated by the majority culture church leaders?	○	○	○
19. Do you know how leaders can be helped to understand one another's different communication and decision-making styles?	○	○	○
20. Do you know how to ensure that leaders and pastors of the different language congregations that might make up a church community operate as a united leadership team?	○	○	○
21. Have you considered how to arrange the teaching? Will all members study the same material in all congregations?	○	○	○

Question	Yes	No	Maybe
22. Can you develop a unified church community when church members belong to separate language and perhaps age congregations?	○	○	○
23. Are you aware of and able to provide ongoing pastoral support and encouragement for those engaged in cross-cultural ministry, including the leaders of particular ethnic churches?	○	○	○
24. Do you know how to go about recruiting leaders for ministry across cultures, including finding pastors for particular ethnic or international congregations?	○	○	○
25. Do you know how to maximise the benefits associated with bringing in a leader from overseas?	○	○	○
26. Do you know how to mitigate the risks associated with bringing in a leader from overseas?	○	○	○
27. Are you aware of how you can go about providing suitable training for potential or existing leaders of particular ethnic or international congregations which takes into account their special needs and limitations?	○	○	○

For the congregation in general

Question	Yes	No	Maybe
28. Do you know how church members can be helped to understand people of other cultures so as to avoid hurtful misunderstandings and value people on their own terms?	○	○	○
29. Do you know how your church can make sure that visitors to the church from different ethnic and cultural backgrounds are welcomed and related to in a culturally sensitive manner?	○	○	○

Questions	Yes	No	Maybe
30. Are you aware of how a church might acquaint itself with the complexities of the current migration and refugee program, in order to be able to offer practical assistance to migrants and refugees?	◯	◯	◯
31. Are your pastors and other leaders already stretched? If so, how can they be best resourced and supported to provide the leadership needed?	◯	◯	◯
32. Are you aware of the kind of agreement that is needed when differing ethnic churches share the church property?	◯	◯	◯
33. Have you considered how the finances will be managed if minority groups meet in and use the church's facilities?	◯	◯	◯
34. Are you aware of the special needs of second generation children and young people, and how you will address them?	◯	◯	◯

For cross-cultural workers in particular

	Yes	No	Maybe
35. Do you know where cross-cultural workers can go to learn relevant local ethnic languages when it is decided that at least some facility in other languages would be helpful?	◯	◯	◯
36. Are you familiar with the supportive structures for ministry across cultures that can be developed both within the church community and the denomination of which the church may be a part?	◯	◯	◯
37. Are you aware of how church workers can come to terms with the challenge of other faiths in the local community and maintain the integrity of the gospel against relativistic and possibly universalistic claims?	◯	◯	◯

Question	Yes	No	Maybe
38. Do you know how leaders and laity in an affiliated ethnic church or group can be helped to understand the culture of the society and church with which they are connected?	○	○	○

For everyone

	Yes	No	Maybe
39. Can you assess your personal working style, aptitudes and interests to help decide your best way of contributing to a ministry across cultures?	○	○	○
40. Do you know what your hesitations are in going into a ministry focused on other cultures?	○	○	○
41. Are you aware that you can seek clarification and the know-how to help you overcome at least some of the barriers that are standing in the way of your engaging in cross-cultural outreach?	○	○	○
42. Do you have a personal plan to look after yourself, even as you seek to look after others?	○	○	○

APPENDIX D: REACHING THE SECOND GENERATION FOR JESUS

There is increasing evidence, factually and anecdotally, that the children of Christian migrants are leaving church life in significant numbers. In the US, this 'silent exodus' claims some 85% of these children upon reaching university age. We in Australia have good reason to suspect that a comparable degree of exodus is happening with our own second generation young people. In a sense this is typical of children of Anglo Aussie Christian parents, as well. However, compared with mainstream Christian families, migrant families face additional difficulties in passing on their faith to the next generation. In recognition of this phenomenon, here are some thoughts on addressing the challenge of reaching the second generation for Jesus.

1. Parenting is not easy and is both an earthly and a spiritual task. Children's experience of discipline in the home shapes their understanding of heavenly discipline and ultimately their understanding and acceptance of the love of Jesus for them. Responsible disciplining of our children is particularly challenging for migrants. Second generation children are profoundly influenced by a different culture from the one in which their parents were raised. So the first and second generation have developed different understandings of what constitutes appropriate discipline. Fortunately, the Bible provides helpful, well-balanced guidance: on the one hand, parents are exhorted to: "Discipline your children ..." (Proverbs 19:18), and on the other hand, they are told, "...do not exasperate your children ..." (Ephesians 6:4).

2. The culture of our second generation children is more than what they inherit from their first generation parents. It is the sum of their parents' cultural background/s and the dominant community's culture. Reaching the second generation means recognising that we have to meander through this cultural divide. Many of the effective strategies for ministry across cultures can be applied to ministry to second generation children. Ying Yee

of a Chinese Christian church in Sydney describes his work amongst the second generation as cross-cultural ministry.

3. Many cross-cultural workers spend time getting to know the people with whom they are building relationships. First generation migrants can easily lose sight of the need to practise this same principle when relating to their children. The pursuit of a good standard of living, and the drive to give to their children what they themselves never had, often cloud their priorities and influence the expectations they have of their children. The resulting problem is often not one of poor communication but of lack of any communication at all, with the resulting lost opportunities to share about Jesus.

4. Engaging with the second generation is usually more effective when led by second generation ministers. Peter Lai of Alhambra True Light Church in the US intentionally nurtured a man 40 years younger than himself to go on and co-pastor with him in a parallel ministry. In this parallel ministry, the first generation and second generation members worship and minister separately, but they come together for some worship services and celebrations, share meals, and have one budget, board and vision.

5. Steve Oh was serving in a Korean church and left for a second generation church plant, Sydney Living Hope Community Church. He advocates for a side by-side model where the first and second generation are in two churches led by their own senior pastors, have separate governance and budgeting structures, and are separately registered within the presbytery/denomination to which they may belong. However, the two churches maintain formal and informal links with one another.

On a positive note, the authors observe that, as minority ethnic churches respond to the 'silent exodus' phenomenon, second generation children, upon leaving the church in which they grew up, don't always simply leave the faith. Some choose to migrate out of their minority culture churches to mainstream culture churches for various reasons. These might include a desire to actively serve in and through those churches. Migrant parents can still feel a sense of great loss even in this instance, especially when their culture is strongly collectivistic. However, communication and continuing

Christian fellowship and care between parents and children can help to smooth this otherwise difficult transition. First generation parents can be helped to see the importance of raising their children with a vision to take the gospel to other cultures.

APPENDIX E: RESOURCES YOU CAN DRAW ON

Websites

Authors' Websites

Andrew Schachtel: www.cultureconnect.net.au

Choon-Hwa Lim: www.psychology.org.au/Lim

Mike Wilson: www.facetofaceintercultural.com.au

Other Websites

5Fish. These are spoken Bible stories and scriptures in many languages, produced by Global Recordings. www.5fish.mobi/au?r=Oceania&country=Australia As well as the site, there is a Five Fish app for both Android and iPhone.

Anglicare ESL Resources: shop.anglicare.org.au/esl/?sort=featured&page=1

Asian Nation. Asian American History, Demographics & Issues. This is a US-focused site, but it contains material which may be useful in the Australian context: www.asian-nation.org/index.shtml.

Aussie ESL. Teaching English, a key that unlocks so many doors: www.aussieesl.com/

Australian Bureau of Statistics. An important source of demographic data for your locality: www.abs.gov.au

Australian Fellowship of Evangelical Students (AFES). AFES is actively involved in international student ministry through its FOCUS program: www.afes.org.au/page/focus

Bible Storytelling Seminars. These are run by Wycliffe Bible Translators Australia (www.wycliffe.org.au) and by a number of other groups.

Easy English Bible Studies. Bible Translation, Bible Commentaries, and Bible Studies in Easy English: www.easyenglish.info/index.htm

Ethnic Harvest. Resources for Multicultural Ministry: www.ethnicharvest.org/

Faith to Faith. This is a UK network, but some of their material and resources may be useful in Australian contexts: www.faithtofaith.org.uk/

God Speaks My Language. This site is designed to help people meet Jesus in their heart language, using their preferred learning method: www.mylanguage. net.au/

Here's Life. This is Campus Crusade Australia's site providing many ideas and resources for cross-cultural ministry: www.hereslife.com/dev/

The Hofstede Centre. Highlights much of Hofstede's work on culture: geert-hofstede.com/geert-hofstede.html

International student information and resources from the Australian Government: www.australia.gov.au/people/students/international-students

International Teams. An organisation that works with refugees and asylum seekers in a variety of ways: www.iteams.org.au/

J. D. Payne. Payne is a US missiologist who writes and blogs on cross-cultural ministry: www.jdpayne.org

Kitab Books. This is an excellent online store for books and other resources in more than 35 languages to help Christians to reach out to peoples of other faiths: www.kitab.org.uk

MisLinks. Connecting you with mission resources: www.mislinks.org/

National Church Life Survey (NCLS). Valuable material to help churches understand their communities: www.ncls.org.au

Peacewise seminars. Useful resources for dealing with conflict in general, including cross-cultural conflict: www.peacewise.org.au

Red Cross Migration Support: www.redcross.org.au/migration-support.aspx

Refugee Council of Australia. Refugee and asylum-seeker information and resources: www.refugeecouncil.org.au/

Refugee Highway. This partnership has a vision to connect the many different people involved in refugee ministry at diverse points around the world: www.refugeehighway.net/

World Bibles. Provides Bibles in over 4000 languages: www.worldbibles.org/search_languages/eng

Videos

Cross-cultural Communication Seminars (Hurstville Presbyterian Church): www.cccseminarsathpc.wordpress.com/

Talk 1 (Andrew Schachtel): What does a multi-ethnic church look like?

Talk 2 (Allan Mao): Who are the people around you? A walk through the neighbourhood.

Talk 3 (Tim & Val Nicholson): How do we develop genuine friendships with migrants?

Talk 4 (John Gill): How do we tell the story of Jesus cross-culturally?

Talk 5 (Mike Wilson): What are the barriers to developing a healthy multi-ethnic ministry?

APPENDIX F: READING LIST

Adibi, H 1998, 'Iranians in Australia', in G Trompf & M Honari (eds) with H Abramian, *Mehregan in Sydney: Proceedings of the seminar in Persian studies during the Mehregan Persian Cultural Festival, Sydney, Australia 28 October – 6 November 1994*, School of Studies in Religion, University of Sydney, with the Persian Cultural Foundation of Australia , Sydney, p. 128.

Arnold, CE 2009, *Powers of darkness. Principalities and powers in Paul's letters.* InterVarsity Press, Downers Grove, IL.

Bounds, EM 1962, *Power through prayer*, Zondervan, Grand Rapids, MI.

Bonhoeffer, D 1965, *Life together*, 6th impression, SCM Press, London.

Bullard, P 2011, *Edmund Burke and the art of rhetoric*, Cambridge University Press, Cambridge.

Dickson, J 2014, *A spectator's guide to world religions: an introduction to the big five*, 3rd edn, Aquila Press, Sydney.

Dillon, C 2012, *Telling the gospel through story: evangelism that keeps hearers wanting more*, InterVarsity Press, Downers Grove, IL.

Donovan, VJ 2001, *Christianity rediscovered: an epistle from the Masai*, SCM Press, Norwich.

Earley, PC, & Ang, S 2003, *Cultural intelligence: individual interactions across cultures*, Stanford University Press, Redwood City, CA.

Elmer, D 1993, *Cross-cultural conflict: building relationships for effective ministry*, InterVarsity Press, Downers Grove, IL.

Elmer, D 2006, *Cross-cultural servanthood: serving the world in Christlike humility*, InterVarsity Press, Downers Grove, IL.

Elmer, D 2009, *Cross-cultural connections: stepping out and fitting in around the world*, InterVarsity Press, Downers Grove, IL.

Emerson, MO 2006, *People of the dream: multiracial congregations in the United States*, Princeton University Press, Princeton, NJ.

Fleming, D 2004, *A different world*, Bridgeway Publications, Brisbane.

Galea, R 2004, *No boundaries: second generation needs new approach*, Sydney Anglicans, viewed 4 May 2016, http://sydneyanglicans.net/blogs/missionthinking/1214a

Guinness, O 2003, *Prophetic untimeliness: a challenge to the idol of relevance*, Baker Books, Ada, MI.

Heywood, D 2003, *Managing Change*, http://www.davidheywood.org/articles/Managing%20Change.pdf

Hiebert, PG 2013, 'Cultural differences and the communication of the gospel' in RD Winter & SC Hawthorne (eds), *Perspectives on the world Christian movement: a reader*, 4th edn, William Carey Library, Pasadena, CA.

Hofstede, G 2001, *Culture's consequences: comparing values, behaviors, institutions and organizations across nation*, 2nd edn, Sage Publications, London.

Hofstede, G, Hofstede, GJ and Minkov, M 2010, *Cultures and organisations: software of the mind*, 3rd edn, McGraw-Hill Education, Columbus, OH.

Houston, J 1994, *Seeds blowing in the wind: review of multicultural ministry & mission*. Anglican Diocese of Melbourne, Melbourne.

Jensen, PF 2004, *Presidential address*, Sydney Anglican Diocesan Secretariat, viewed 3 May 2016, http://www.sds.asn.au/site/100821.asp?ph=sy

KU Work Group for Community Health and Development. (2015). Chapter 3, Section 1: *Developing a Plan for Assessing Local Needs and Resources*. Lawrence, KS: University of Kansas. Retrieved January 9, 2015, from the Community Tool Box: http://ctb.ku.edu/en/table-of-contents/assessment/assessing-community-needs-and-resources/develop-a-plan/main

Lane, D 2008, *One world two minds: eastern and western outlooks in a changing world*, OMF International, Littleton, CO.

Lane, P 2002, *A beginner's guide to crossing cultures: making friends in a multicultural world*, InterVarsity Press, Downers Grove, IL.

Lausanne Committee for World Evangelization 2005, *The new people next door: a call to seize the opportunities*, Lausanne Occasional Paper No. 55, viewed 20 July 2016, https://www.lausanne.org/wp-content/uploads/2007/06/LOP55_IG26.pdf

Lingenfelter, S, & Mayers, M 2003, *Ministering cross-culturally: an incarnational model for personal relationships*, Baker Academic, Ada, MI.

Loewen, JA 2000, *The Bible in cross-cultural perspective*, William Carey Library,

Pasadena CA.

McLure Mudge, J 2015, 'Emerson's legacy in America', in J McLure Mudge (ed.), *Mr Emerson's Revolution*, Open Book Publishers, Cambridge, UK. http://dx.doi.org/10.11647/OBP.0065).

Mencken, HL 1956, *Minority report*. H. L. Mencken's notebooks, Alfred A. Knopf, NY.

Milne, B 2008, *Dynamic diversity: bridging class, age, race and gender in the church*, Inter-Varsity Press, Downers Grove, IL.

NSW Migration Heritage Centre 2011, *A new life in Blacktown*, Blacktown City Council, viewed 28 June 2016, http://www.migrationheritage.nsw.gov.au/exhibition/sudanesestories/edward-massimino/index.html

Payne, JD 2012, *Strangers next door: immigration, migration and mission*, InterVarsity Press, Downers Grove, IL.

Percy, N 2008, *Honours list rewards Sydney servant*, Sydney Anglicans, viewed 3 May 2016, http://sydneyanglicans.net/news/honours_list_recognises_sydney_servant

Peterson, B 2011, *Cultural intelligence: a guide to working with people from other cultures*, Nicholas Brealey Publishing, London.

Piper, J 2010. *Let the nations be glad!: the supremacy of God in missions*, Baker Academic, Grand Rapids, MI.

Reeder, HL III & Swavely, D 2008, *From embers to a flame. How God can revitalize your church*, Presbyterian & Reformed Publishing Company, Phillipsburg, NJ.

Rhodes, S 1998, *Where the nations meet: the church in a multicultural world*, InterVarsity Press, Downers Grove, IL.

Roland, A 2003, 'Psychoanalysis across civilizations: a personal journey', *Journal of the American Academy of Psychoanalysis and Dynamic Psychiatry*, vol. 31, no. 2, pp. 275-295.

Sire, JW 2009, *The universe next door: a basic worldview catalogue*, 5th edn, Intervarsity Press Academic, Downers Grove, IL.

Storti, C 1994, *Cross-cultural dialogues: 74 brief encounters with cultural difference*, Intercultural Press, Boston, MA.

Thew, J 1996, *Easy English Worship*, Anglicare, Diocese of Sydney, ESL Ministry, Parramatta.

Tow, V 2009, *Background to Indian culture and Hinduism*, Anglicare, Diocese of Sydney, ESL Ministry, Parramatta.

Tow, V 2010, *Background to Chinese culture and religions*, Anglicare, Diocese of Sydney, ESL Ministry, Parramatta.

Wilson, A 2008, *ESL classes reveal buried treasure*, Sydney Anglicans, viewed 2 May 2016, http://sydneyanglicans.net/news/esl_classes_reveal_buried_treasure sydneyanglicans.net

Witherington, B III 2009, *Imminent domain: the story of the kingdom of God and its celebration*, Wm B. Eerdmans, Grand Rapids, MI.

Wright, CJH 2006, *The mission of God: unlocking the Bible's grand narrative*, InterVarsity Press Academic, Downers Grove, IL.

Wright, CJH 2010, *The mission of God's people: a biblical theology of the church's mission*, Zondervan, Grand Rapids, MI.

Lightning Source UK Ltd.
Milton Keynes UK
UKOW01f2345220817
307738UK00002B/386/P